MACHINE-QUILTING
IDEA BOOK

61 Designs to Finish Classic Patchwork

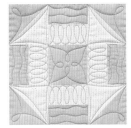 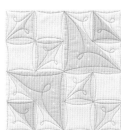  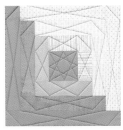 

Vicki Ruebel

Martingale®
Create with Confidence

Machine-Quilting Idea Book:
61 Designs to Finish Classic Patchwork
© 2019 by Vicki Ruebel

Martingale®
19021 120th Ave. NE, Ste. 102
Bothell, WA 98011-9511 USA
ShopMartingale.com

Printed in China
24 23 22 21 20 19   8 7 6 5 4 3 2 1

Library of Congress Cataloging-in-Publication Data
Names: Ruebel, Vicki, author.
Title: Machine-quilting idea book : 61 designs to finish classic patchwork / by Vicki Ruebel.
Description: Bothell, WA : Martingale, [2019] | Summary: "Quilters often ask, "How should I quilt this quilt?" This book answers that question by showing 12 commonly used quilt blocks and providing six quilting designs for each block. The designs for each block progress in complexity, but with a little practice, quilters will be able to achieve any of them."—Provided by publisher.
Identifiers: LCCN 2019026077 | ISBN 9781683560418 (paperback)
Subjects: LCSH: Patchwork--Patterns. | Machine quilting— Patterns.
Classification: LCC TT835 .R84 2019 | DDC 746.46/041—dc23
LC record available at https://lccn.loc.gov/2019026077

MISSION STATEMENT

We empower makers who use fabric and yarn
to make life more enjoyable.

CREDITS

**PUBLISHER AND
CHIEF VISIONARY OFFICER**
Jennifer Erbe Keltner

CONTENT DIRECTOR
Karen Costello Soltys

DESIGN MANAGER
Adrienne Smitke

MANAGING EDITOR
Tina Cook

PRODUCTION MANAGER
Regina Girard

**ACQUISITIONS AND
DEVELOPMENT EDITOR**
Laurie Baker

PHOTOGRAPHER
Brent Kane

TECHNICAL EDITOR
Nancy Mahoney

ILLUSTRATOR
Sandy Loi

COPY EDITOR
Melissa Bryan

Contents

Quilting on Patchwork Blocks

A Quilting Path

The question I'm asked most often—and I'm pretty sure it's a question that most quilters ask themselves even if they don't say it out loud—is, "How should I quilt this quilt?"

My goal in writing this book was to create an encyclopedia of designs that all quilters could use for inspiration. Trying to decide on a quilting design can be overwhelming to the point that we feel paralyzed and unable to move forward. When I began quilting in 2010, I'd stare at quilt tops for days trying to figure out what I was doing. More times than not I would end up walking away because I just didn't know where to begin. As time went on, the process became easier for me, and I'm hoping I can help make your journey easier too.

Quite often, books about machine quilting focus on quilting plain, solid fabric. That approach makes it easy to see the designs, but it doesn't help us figure out what to quilt on top of patchwork. This book contains 12 commonly used quilt blocks with four to six quilting designs for each block, for a total of 61 designs. The designs for each block progress in complexity, but with a little practice, you'll be able to achieve any of them. To help you decide where to start, the designs are rated with one, two, or three spools, with one spool being the easiest, two spools being a little more adventurous, and three spools being the most intricate. I hesitate to say "hard" or "challenging" or "advanced," as we all have our own comfort levels and we all learn at different rates of speed. You may be willing to jump right into a three-spool design with all the confidence of an experienced quilter, even if you're just starting out. The spools are just an easy way for you to see at a glance which designs may take a bit more time to master.

If you're a beginning quilter, I recommend starting with the one-spool designs and progressing from there. Experienced quilters may decide to skip over the more basic designs, but I encourage you all to browse through them because sometimes simple designs can be a nice way to complete a quilt quickly. All types of quilters, whether you quilt on a home sewing machine or a long-arm machine, will be able to use these designs.

Don't let the fear of messing up your quilt paralyze you. I promise, no one has ever messed up his or her quilt so severely with quilting that it can't be fixed. It's not going to self-combust if your quilting isn't perfect. The worst-case scenario is that you may need to rip out a few stitches. That's OK. It's also completely normal to feel like you have to force yourself to start, but don't worry—I've always found that the ideas begin to flow once I take that first step.

How to Use This Book

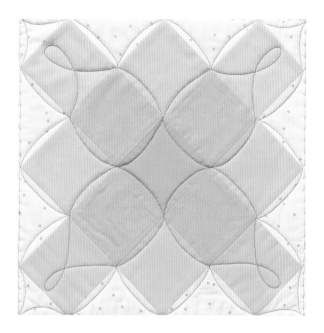

As I mentioned in the introduction, there are 12 patchwork block designs in this book, and each one offers different quilting ideas. But before you dive in, especially if you're new to machine quilting, take a look at what the designs encompass.

One-Spool Designs

All the designs marked with a single spool icon are perfectly suited toward beginners. The designs are not very dense and are easy to execute. You won't have to worry about starting and stopping because I show you how to move around the block with the designs. Keep in mind: I love to travel (that is, move the machine needle from one point to another) by stitching in the seamlines to move around the block. I've been doing this for years, and it works great. Most people are scared to travel around the block, but it makes life so much easier.

Marking the quilt top is not required for any of the one-spool designs, but do not hesitate to mark things if you find it helpful. When I first started quilting, I used a water-soluble Mark-B-Gone pen all the time. I'm a huge advocate of making life easier, so if marking does that, then mark up your quilt tops! The designs in the one-spool category include continuous curves, wavy lines, organic crosshatching, loops, and a few more. Once you become familiar with these simple designs, they should be pretty fast to execute. I love quilting that I can do quickly and without too much thinking.

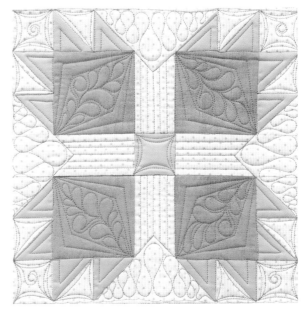

Two-Spool Designs

Designs noted with the two-spool icon build upon the one-spool designs and stretch your creativity. They may be a little challenging and take more practice, but don't be intimidated. You can do it! I tried to minimize starts and stops within this category, but a few blocks do have them. This just means you can't complete the entire block in one pass. You'll need to do more marking in this category as we break up the blocks into smaller sections. I love using this technique for quilting because it helps me tackle larger areas. The designs in the intermediate category include all the motifs from the easier category plus swirls, feathers, pebbles, double continuous curves layered with other designs, ribbon candy, and more. These designs definitely take longer to execute, so keep that in mind if you're quilting a king-size quilt. I don't recommend pebbling a king-size quilt; you'll be cross-eyed and saying bad things about me.

Three-Spool Designs

Three-spool designs are more advanced. They will definitely challenge you (which is a good thing), but they are totally doable. Just remember: practice, practice, practice. I can't say that enough.

There are starts and stops in this category and lots of marking. I let you know when it's time to "stop and tie off." Keep in mind that you can decide exactly how you want to do that. You can tie knots in the thread tails and then bury them, or take several small stitches and then snip the thread tails. This is a matter of personal preference, so do what works best for you. I do a bit of both depending on which method will work best for the quilt I'm making.

This category includes everything from the one- and two-spool categories plus grid work, ruler work, and even more feathers. These designs are the most time consuming because they are very dense, but in my opinion, they're totally worth it! Again, maybe you don't want to start with a king-size quilt to try out these designs. Choose a smaller project and work your way up to something on a larger scale.

Using the Right Tools

With quilting, as with any activity, having the right tools makes a huge difference. In this section I'll share a few of my favorites and explain why I love them and how to use them. I recommend adding these items to your quilting toolbox so that you're always prepared to tackle new projects.

Plexiglas and Dry Erase Marker

An acrylic plastic Plexiglas sheet and a dry erase marker are probably my favorite design tools. Run to your local hardware store and buy a piece of Plexiglas right now! Make sure you wrap the edges with duct tape for visibility so that you don't draw off the Plexiglas onto your quilt. I personally love sparkly glitter duct tape, but you can use any color.

The piece of Plexiglas I use is approximately 14" × 24", but you can use any size that works for you. The beauty of Plexiglas is that it allows you to try out quilting designs before you stitch anything. Lay the Plexiglas on top of your quilt and use a dry erase marker to practice drawing the quilt design. You can find the quilting path and practice until you feel comfortable actually doing it. This is much more efficient than what I used to do. I would start quilting, hope for the best, and do lots of ripping when I didn't like the results. Now I use my Plexiglas and dry erase marker to eliminate the guesswork. I prefer this method to taking a picture and drawing on the photo, because with Plexiglas I can see my designs in the correct scale.

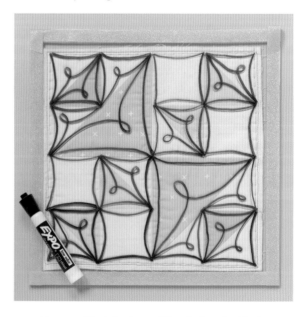

Use your Plexiglas to audition designs for blocks and figure out your quilting path. Apply tape to make the edges of the Plexiglas clearly visible.

Thread

I love thread, and I encourage you to have fun playing with different types. The thread weight plays an important role when quilting. For example, the more advanced quilting designs are very dense and can be overwhelming if not handled properly. I suggest using a thinner thread for very dense designs. My personal favorites are 100-weight silk, 100-weight Microquilter, and 50-weight So Fine. For everyday use, my go-to combination is Superior Thread's Omni (40-weight) for the top thread and Bottom Line (60-weight) in the bobbin. I do use Omni for denser quilting, but I'm mindful that it can build up quickly if I have to go over something more than once.

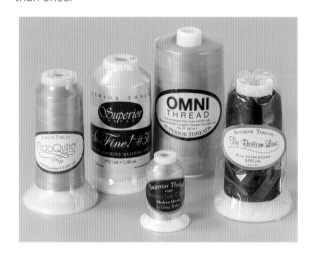

Different threads produce different effects, so experiment to find your favorites.

For the samples in this book, I used a very dark Omni thread to make the quilting easy to see. In real life, however, I don't normally use such a high-contrast thread. There are exceptions to this rule, but in general I prefer a matching or blending thread because I find the effect much more pleasing.

I selected one of the Churn Dash blocks with an advanced quilting design for the following examples. I quilted the block once with dark thread and again with matching thread to illustrate what a huge difference thread color can make. On the block with dark thread, shown in the upper-right photo, the thread overpowers the pebbles. It's obvious when the backtracking isn't perfectly

executed. I would never use such a high-contrast thread for this type of quilting. The dark thread takes away from the texture that is created by the pebble quilting. You focus more on the thread color than on the actual design.

Block quilted with dark thread

In the photo below, see what a difference matching thread makes! The same quilting looks totally different. You can't tell my pebbles aren't perfect; instead, you see the texture. Thread color should never overpower your fabrics. You want to choose colors that complement your fabrics so the quilting is pleasing, not overpowering. This is definitely the better version of this block.

Block quilted with matching thread

Finally, I tend to favor light thread on dark fabric as opposed to dark thread on light fabric. This all comes down to personal preference, though, so what works for me may be different for you. I suggest playing with practice quilt sandwiches and testing out different brands, colors, and weights of thread. Don't be afraid to try new things. Just remember, you may need to adjust your machine's tension when changing thread weights.

Marking Pen and Pencil

My favorite marking pen is a Dritz Mark-B-Gone water-soluble pen. I've never had any issues with the marks not coming out, although sometimes I have to spritz the marks more than once. You can also wash your quilt after it's quilted to remove the marks. I prefer to finish the quilting, lay the quilt out flat, spritz it with water, and let it air dry. This method works great for me. For marking dark fabrics, I use a General's white chalk pencil.

I highly recommend using these tools when you're a new quilter. I used to have trouble visualizing the designs on my quilts, so I would draw the beginning of the design. That was just enough to help me start and get over my fear of quilting. Do what works for you and don't worry about the rest.

Mark-B-Gone water-soluble pen and General's white chalk pencil.

Ruler Quilting

For a few of the blocks, such as the Log Cabin block on page 27, I used a straight-edge quilting ruler. This type of ruler allows me to quilt straight, evenly spaced lines. Although there are many different rulers that can be used to create a million different

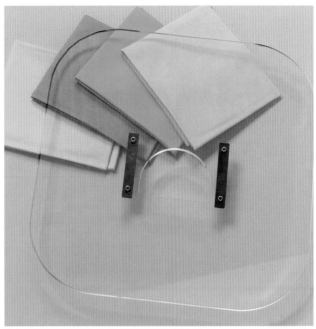

Tools for ruler quilting: Creative Grids quilting ruler (left), Innova ruler foot (upper middle),
Bernina adjustable ruler foot #72 (lower middle), Innova ruler plate for long-arm machine (right).

shapes, I suggest starting with a straight ruler to make sure you enjoy ruler quilting before buying all the rulers. Keep in mind, ruler quilting takes quite a bit longer to accomplish than quilting without the aid of a ruler.

When quilting with a ruler, only use rulers that are ¼" thick. Thinner rulers made for cutting fabric are not effective for quilting and should be avoided.

Whether using a domestic or a long-arm machine, you'll need a ruler foot. A ruler foot has a taller lip so that you don't run over your ruler. Stitching over a ruler can break the ruler, knock the machine out of time, and even rip a hole in the quilt. When using rulers, it's important to pay extremely close attention to avoid accidents. Most sewing-machine companies make a ruler foot that will fit each specific machine. There are also generic ruler feet, but I recommend getting a foot made especially for your machine, if available.

I use an Innova ruler foot for most of my long-arm quilting. I'm a bit lazy and don't like changing my foot, so I leave my ruler foot on all the time. It works just fine for all my quilting and saves me a little time because I don't have to worry about changing feet.

When doing ruler work with a long-arm machine, use an extended base so that you have a place to rest the ruler. Without the base, it's easy to tip the ruler and accidentally hit it with the needle. If your long-arm machine doesn't come with an extended base, you'll need to purchase one.

Sandwich Prep

Have you fallen out of love with some of the fabrics in your stash? Turn them into small quilt sandwiches so that you can practice your quilting. Piece blocks or simply cut squares and layer them with batting and a backing fabric, then start quilting and watch your skills advance!

Overview of Quilting Designs

Before we delve into the individual blocks and their quilting options, let's go over a few of the basic quilting designs. I recommend grabbing some paper and doing a little doodling if you are new to these designs. I love to practice before I try to quilt new designs. Drawing first helps my brain understand what I need to do to execute the design once I start quilting. Don't worry if you can't draw. I can't draw either. I simply do my best, and I know that if I can kind of get the design on paper, I can quilt it. I know it sounds strange, but I promise it works. I also love to doodle on my iPad. I use the Adobe Sketch app, which works great.

Continuous Curved Lines

I use continuous curved lines a lot when I quilt. They are a super fun design and great for beginners, but you can fancy them up when you're ready. The hardest part is not boxing yourself into a corner or forgetting a section as you go. To help combat this, I like to work from left to right and top to bottom. It's amazing how fast I can get turned around if I try to stitch in a different direction. I've conditioned my brain into going the same way for so long, I could do these in my sleep. Keep in mind that you may work better right to left or bottom to top, and that's OK. Do what works best for you, but try to be consistent in order to build muscle memory.

I also talk to myself as I quilt. I know it sounds crazy and my hubby loves to poke fun at me about it, but it's a great way to stay on track. When quilting, I'm saying, "over, down, up, over, down, up, over, down, across, across, across." The most important thing with continuous curves is to not quilt all four sides of the square. You need to stitch three sides of the square first. The fourth side is stitched when you travel back to the beginning of the row. Then you move on to the next square.

1. Begin in the top-left corner and stitch to the right, down, and then up. Continue this all the way across the block.

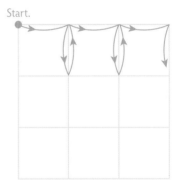

Start.

2. Close the squares by stitching back to the left.

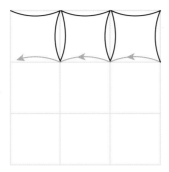

3. Repeat steps 1 and 2 to stitch each row of squares. Then stitch back up to where you started.

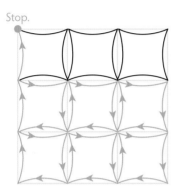

This design works on squares, triangles, diamonds, and basically any other shape you can think of. I suggest practicing continuous curved lines with your Plexiglas and dry erase marker. You can test your muscle memory before trying to quilt them. It's much easier to erase stitches than to rip them out.

To stitch double curved lines, I create two curved lines. The additional line adds a little extra texture. I love mixing single curved lines with double curved lines just for fun. Don't be afraid to try new things.

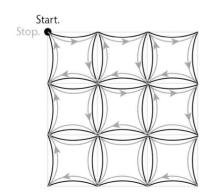

Swirls

Swirls are my favorite quilting design. I'm pretty sure I put them on just about everything. I like to create little bubbles in the center of my swirls, and it's fine if yours look a little different. I used to beat myself up because I couldn't get my swirls to look like everyone else's. Then I realized I should focus on making the best swirls I can. We all have different signatures, so our quilting is going to be unique as well. Don't stress about trying to match my style exactly; just look at how I construct the design and then make it your own.

1. Starting along one edge, stitch a rounded line upward and then curl down into the center of the swirl. Echo stitch the inside of the swirl and curl out of the swirl.

2. Repeat to stitch a second swirl and then a third.

3. If you stitch yourself into a corner or end up with odd-shaped areas that need to be filled in, echo stitch your way out by following the shape of the swirl. This is a good way to fill in areas that aren't large enough for a whole swirl.

Echo stitching to fill odd shapes.

Feathers

Feathers were one of the most difficult designs for me to learn but totally worth the effort and hours of practice. I make all of my feathers from the bottom to the top because when I try to make them from the top down it looks like I was quilting while tipsy. Sometimes I quilt the spine first, but not often. My feathers usually start small, get a little bigger toward the middle, and then get smaller again toward the top. Don't be afraid to stretch your plumes to make them fit the shape of the area.

1. Begin by stitching a teardrop shape. Add a plume beside the teardrop. Continue adding plumes until the feather is complete.

Start.

2. To stitch inside a triangle, start in one of the small corners and stitch a teardrop. Add a plume above the teardrop. Continue stitching plumes, stretching them into the corner to fill the entire space. Then stitch smaller plumes to complete the feather. The long side of the triangle acts as the spine of the feather.

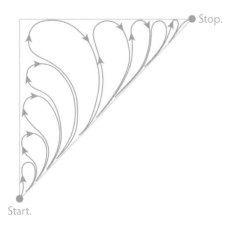

Stop.

Start.

3. Add a little flare every now and then by stitching an extra plume, loop, or swirl inside some of the plumes. I do this randomly as I stitch, whenever I feel like giving a plume a bit of extra interest.

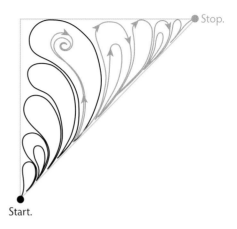

Stop.

Start.

Pebbles

Pebbles are a great way to add texture to your quilts. Be aware that they take a long time to quilt, so start out small and work your way up to larger areas. My best tip for quilting nice, round pebbles is to switch stitching direction with each pebble.

I like to vary the size of the pebbles. If I try to make them all uniform, it's too noticeable when one is accidentally very large or teeny-tiny. When the pebbles are various sizes, I find it much easier to relax and have fun. Also, I'm not overly concerned about making sure I stitch exactly on the previous line of stitching, which is called backtracking. It's almost impossible to make precise pebbles, and honestly no one will ever notice if your backtracking isn't perfect. This is especially true if you use matching thread, which I highly recommend when quilting pebbles.

It's also fun to add a little flare to your pebbles by quilting swirls inside a few of them.

1. Stitch the first pebble in a clockwise direction. Stitch the second pebble in a counterclockwise direction.

2. Continue stitching pebbles, alternating the direction and varying the size of the pebbles.

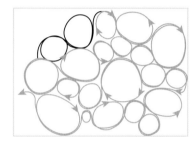

3. As you stitch the pebbles, randomly stitch a swirl in a few pebbles to add a little flare.

Alternating the stitching direction is important because otherwise your pebbles will look like little eyeglasses. Plus, the pebbles will most likely wind up being in a row, making it harder to fill the space as needed.

Ribbon Candy

Ribbon Candy is a versatile pattern that can be used to fill just about any shape.

1. Stitch a curl counterclockwise and then stitch upward to the left. Stitch a clockwise curl. Stitch down and to the left, brushing the previous line of stitching. Stitch counterclockwise to begin an upward curl.

2. Continue stitching the curl to the left, brushing the previous line of stitching.

Quilting on Patchwork Blocks

Each of the traditional blocks is shown quilted several different ways, with options for beginners, options that are a bit more challenging, and options that are more advanced. With every option you will see the quilted block as well as an illustration of the quilting path to follow in order to complete the design.

Courthouse Steps BLOCKS

The "steps" in the Courthouse Steps block are ideal for quilting rings around the center. Use the steps to help define the space in the block and add all kinds of fun quilting.

OPTION 1

1. Starting at the lower-left corner of the longest dark rectangle, stitch a wavy line to the top of the rectangle. Travel stitch about ¼" to the right. Stitch a wavy line to the bottom of the rectangle. In the same way, stitch two or three wavy lines in each of the dark rectangles on the left side of the block (purple).

2. When you reach the center square, stitch four vertical wavy lines through the square. Then stitch two or three wavy lines in each of the dark rectangles on the right side of the block (green).

3. When you reach the outer edge of the block, travel stitch along the outer edges until you reach the top-left corner of the top outermost light rectangle. Stitch horizontal wavy lines in each of the light rectangles. Stitch horizontal lines through the center square to create a crosshatched grid. Then stitch wavy lines in each of the remaining light rectangles (red).

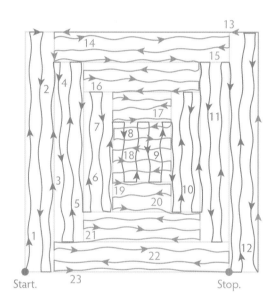

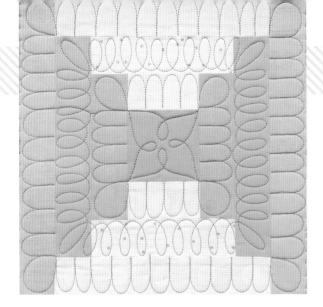

OPTION 2

1. Starting at the top-left corner of the center square, stitch loops around the center square. When you reach the starting point, stitch humps in the innermost ring of rectangles, adding a loop in each corner (purple).

2. When you reach the starting point, stitch in the ditch to the middle ring of rectangles. Stitch loops around the middle ring back to where you started (green).

3. Travel stitch to the outer ring of rectangles. Stitch humps in the outermost ring of rectangles, adding a loop in each corner (red).

Keep Moving

You don't need to stop and tie off as you move from one round to the next, especially if you use matching thread. The stitching is more noticeable with high-contrast thread, but I'd rather move around my block and not tie off whenever possible.

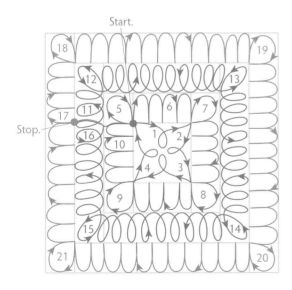

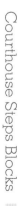

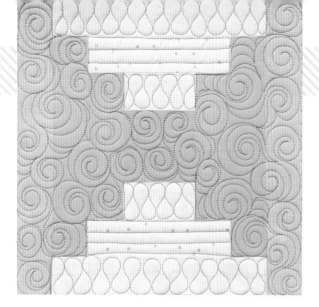

OPTION 3

1. Starting at the top-left corner of the top outermost light rectangle, stitch ribbon candy through the rectangle from left to right. (See "Ribbon Candy" on page 15.) Stitch in the ditch to the top-right corner of the next light rectangle. Stitch straight lines back and forth, ending in the lower-left corner. Stitch in the ditch to the top-left corner of the next light rectangle. Stitch ribbon candy in the inner-most light rectangle, working from left to right (purple).

2. When you reach the top-right corner of the light rectangle, stitch swirls in the dark rectangles and through the center square. If you back yourself into a corner while stitching the swirls, echo stitch your way out. Travel stitch as needed to end the swirls in the top-right corner of the bottom innermost light rectangle (green).

3. In the same way as before, stitch ribbon candy in the innermost light rectangle, straight lines in the middle rectangle, and ribbon candy in the outermost rectangle (red).

Start.

Stop.

OPTION 4

1. Draw a V shape from the outermost corners of the light rectangle to the center square. Repeat to mark a V on the opposite side of the block (blue lines). Starting at the inner point of the V and using one line as the spine, stitch feathers up both sides of one line. Echo stitch around the bottom side of the plumes. Travel stitch as needed to the starting point. Stitch feathers up the other marked line and echo stitch around the plumes. Be sure to stitch loops above and below the starting point (purple). Tie off. Repeat to stitch feathers on the opposite side of the block (green). Tie off.

2. Using a ruler and working from the outer edge toward the center, stitch parallel straight lines about ½" apart. Travel stitch along the echo lines to stitch the next straight line. When you reach the center, stop and tie off or travel stitch to the other side by stitching over the echo lines. Then stitch straight lines on the other side of the block (red).

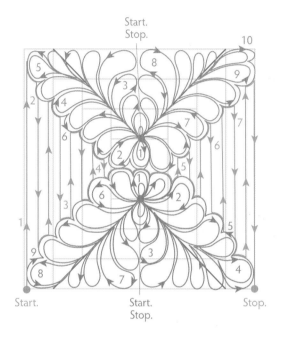

Echo the Plumes

The echo stitching helps differentiate the plumes from the rest of the quilting. You'll use it for traveling later on.

Log Cabin BLOCKS

Log Cabin blocks are perfect for all types of quilting! Use the logs as placement guides for feathers, swirls, and straight lines. Let your imagination flow!

OPTION 1

1. Position the block so that the darker fabrics are on the left and bottom edges. Starting at the top-left corner of the block, stitch a curved line to the lower-left corner. Stitch a curved line up to the top-right corner of the next log. Stitch a curved line back down to the lower-left corner. Stitch a curved line up to the top-right corner of the third log and back down to the lower-left corner. Stitch a curved line to the top-right corner of the center square and back to the corner of the block. Stitch curved lines in the next two logs in the same way. In the last log, stitch a curved line from the lower-left corner to the lower-right corner (green).

2. Travel stitch to the light log. Stitch in the ditch between the light and dark logs ⅛" to ¼". Stitch a wavy line to the top-right corner and then stitch to the top-left corner of the light log. Stitch in the ditch about ½". Stitch a wavy line back to the right and then down to the end of the light log. Continue in the same way, stitching two or three wavy lines in each light log (red).

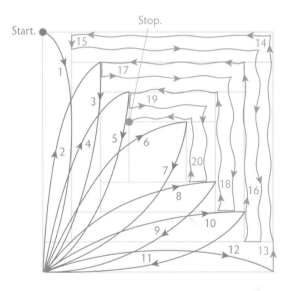

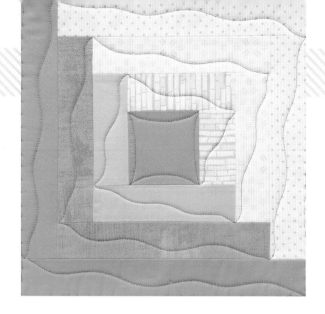

OPTION 2

1. Starting at the lower-right corner of the center square, stitch a continuous curved line around the inside of the square (green).

2. Working in a counterclockwise direction, stitch a wavy line from the lower-left corner to the top-right corner of the first log. In the next log, stitch a wavy line from the lower-right corner to the top-left corner. Continue stitching diagonal wavy lines in each log as you spiral around the block toward the lower-right corner of the last log (red).

Wavy Lines

Wavy lines are perfect for beginners. You don't have to worry about precision, and added texture is easily achieved.

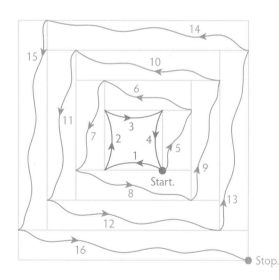

Draw the Spine

You don't have to draw the spine for the feathers, but if you're new to feathers, you may find it helpful to do so. When I want the feathers to fit a certain area, I often find it's easier to follow a line.

OPTION 3

1. Using the seamline as a guide, draw a line at the end of each dark log to create a small square. On the light side of the block, draw an arc that curves toward the center (blue lines).

2. Using the drawn line as the spine, stitch feathers (see "Feathers" on page 14) on both sides of the marked arc. Stretch the plumes as needed to fill the light logs, adding an extra plume in a few of the feathers. When you reach the end of the feather, travel stitch back down the spine to the starting point (top, purple).

3. Using the marked lines as a guide and working diagonally from the starting point to the lower-right corner of the block, stitch continuous curved lines along the top and right side of each of the squares, including the center square (top, green). When you reach the square in the lower-right corner, stitch around the square twice to create a double curved line inside the square. Continue in the same way, stitching double curved lines in each square as you work back to the starting point (top, red).

4. Travel stitch around the top-left corner. Starting below the double curved line, stitch swirls to fill in the dark side of the block (bottom, red).

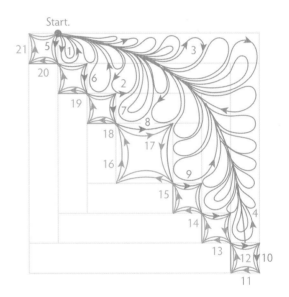

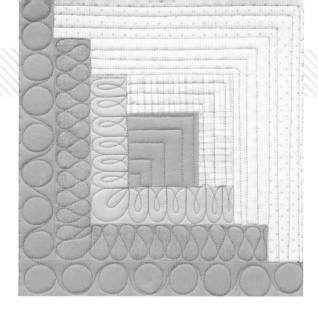

3. Stitch in the ditch until you reach the top-right corner of the next dark log. Working downward and to the right, stitch ribbon candy (page 15) inside the logs (bottom, green).

4. Stitch in the ditch to the top-right corner of the outer dark log. Working to the left and upward, stitch a continuous line of circles in the outer logs (bottom, red).

OPTION 4

1. Starting at the top-left corner of the first light log, stitch a straight line to the top-right corner. Pivot and then stitch down to the end of the light log to create an L shape. Stitch in the ditch about ¼". Stitch a straight line up to the corner and then pivot left to stitch to the end of the light log. Continue, stitching three to four straight lines per log. Stitch straight lines in the center square in the same way until you reach the lower-left corner of the square (top, purple). I did not use a ruler, but you could. Or stitch slightly wavy lines (instead of straight lines) to make it easier.

2. When you reach the lower-left corner of the center square, stitch in the ditch until you reach the top-right corner of the dark log. Stitch humps in the two innermost logs, adding a loop in the corner (top, green). Working in the opposite direction, stitch a small loop inside each hump and in the corner loop (top, red).

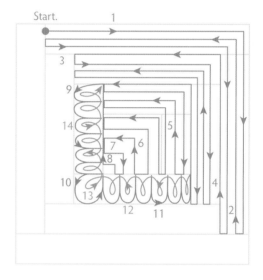

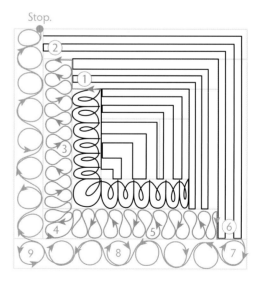

OPTION 5

1. Mark the center point on each side of the center square. Starting at the lower-right corner of the center square and using a ruler, stitch a straight line from the corner to the center point at the top of the square. Stitch to the lower-left corner and to the center point on the right side of the square. Continue spiraling around the square until the star is completed (top, purple).

2. When you are back to the starting point, stitch a diagonal line through the light log to the top-right corner of the log. Stitch a short diagonal line to the point that is opposite the corner of the center square. The length of the line should be the same as the width of the log. If you find it easier, you can mark the side of the log using the seamline as a guide (top, purple).

3. Stitch a diagonal line to the top-left corner of the center square. Stitch a diagonal line through the dark log to the lower-left corner of the log. Stitch a short diagonal line to the point that is opposite the corner of the center square. Stitch a diagonal line through the dark log back to the starting point (top, purple). Tie off.

4. Starting at the lower-right corner of the innermost light log, stitch a diagonal line to the top-left corner of the same log. Stitch a diagonal line to the top-left corner of the next light log. Stitch a short line across the corner of the dark log and then stitch a diagonal line to the lower-right corner of the same log. Continue as before to create a second ring in the inner round of logs (top, green). At the starting point, stop and tie off.

5. Working in a counterclockwise direction, repeat the process to stitch two sets of stitch lines in each round of logs (top, red; bottom, all lines). Tie off when you return to each starting point.

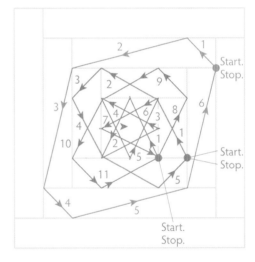

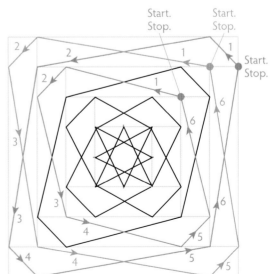

Nine Patch BLOCKS

The Nine Patch block is one of the simplest patchwork blocks, but it offers much versatility for quilting. You can easily use the seamlines as guides for grid quilting or to create lovely secondary designs.

OPTION 1

1. Starting at the top-left corner of the block, stitch a continuous curved line to the top-right corner of the square. Then stitch to the bottom-right corner and pause.

2. Following the sequence numbered below, in the next square, stitch a loop that starts at the lower-left corner and ends at the bottom-right corner; pause.

3. Stitch curved lines on all sides of the top-right square and the center square. Stitch a loop in the middle-right square. Continue moving around the block until you reach the starting point.

Just for Fun

Feel free to mix and match designs. Maybe you like an element from one of the Churn Dash blocks and want to mix it with something from a Double X block. Go for it!

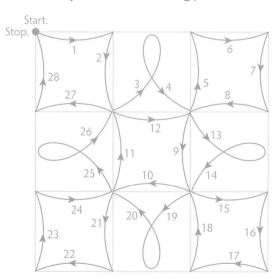

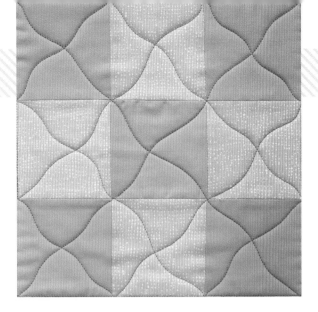

OPTION 2

1. Starting at the lower-left corner of the top-left square, stitch a wavy line to the top-right corner of the square. Travel stitch (stitch in the ditch of the seamline) along the top of the middle square and then stitch a diagonal wavy line down to the top-left corner of the lower-left square. Travel stitch to reach the lower-left corner of the block (red).

2. Stitch a diagonal wavy line up to the top-right corner of the block. Travel stitch down to the top-right corner of the next square. Then stitch a diagonal wavy line down to the lower-left corner of the bottom-middle square (red).

3. Travel stitch across the bottom of the square to the lower-left corner of the last square. Stitch a wavy diagonal line up to the top-right corner of the square. Travel stitch up to the lower-right corner of the top-right square (red).

4. Repeat the entire process, working across the block in the diagonally opposite direction (green).

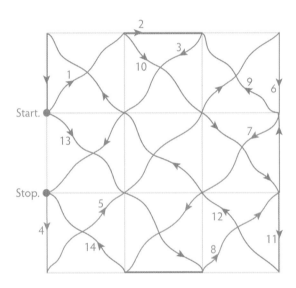

Ride the Wave

Speaking from my own experience, wavy lines are a great option when you are new to quilting. They are easier to stitch than straight lines because if you wobble, it simply becomes part of the design. Wavy lines add great texture to your quilt with a lot less worry.

OPTION 3

1. Starting at the lower-left corner of the top-left square, stitch a continuous curved line up the left side, across the top, and down the right side of the square. When you reach the lower-right corner, stitch into the center square. Stitch a curved line around the center square twice to create a double curved line (top, green).

2. From the top-left corner of the center square, stitch a curved line along the bottom edge of the top-left square. Stitch a second curved line inside the square to create a double curved line. Stitch figure eights inside the curved lines to reach the top-right corner of the square (top, red).

3. In the top-middle square, stitch a slightly curved line down to the center of the seamline and then back up to the top-right corner of the square. (I didn't mark the center; I simply eyeballed it. Feel free to mark the center of the square if you'd like the line to be perfectly centered.)

4. Continue in the same way to work completely around the block (bottom, red).

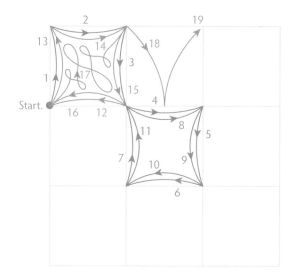

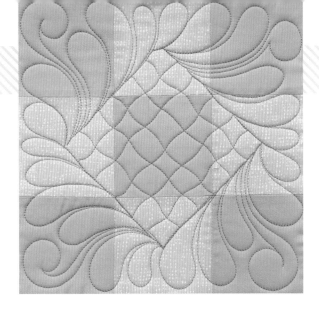

OPTION 4

1. Draw an on-point square in the center of the block, using the corners of the center square as a guide. It isn't necessary to stitch on the drawn line before beginning the feathers. Starting at the left corner of the marked square, stitch feathers into each corner of the block, circling around the marked square (top right). If you don't stretch the feathers into the corners, the block will look somewhat unfinished and awkward. I mixed in a swirl plume to add interest to the design. (See "Feathers" on page 14.)

2. When you reach the starting point, travel stitch about ½" on the marked line. Stitch a wavy grid in the center of the on-point square, stitching five lines in one direction and then stitching five lines in the other direction (bottom right). Stop and tie off. I didn't mark the grid because I love organic quilting. However, you might find it helpful to mark the grid lines.

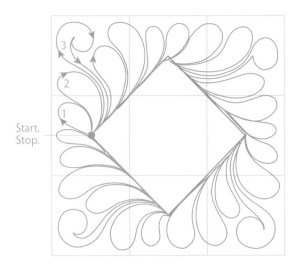

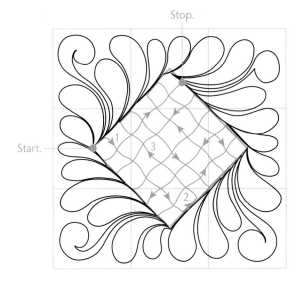

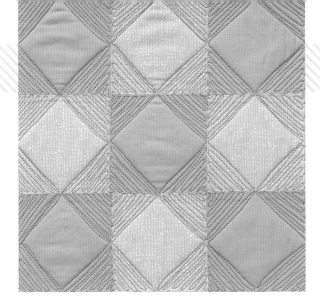

OPTION 5

1. Draw a grid that divides each patchwork square into four smaller squares. Starting at the top-left corner, stitch closely spaced diagonal lines to fill the top half of the small square. Move to the next small square and stitch from the marked line to the bottom-right corner. You will alternate quilting from the outside in and inside out as you work your way across the block. Continue in the same way until you reach the end of the top row (top).

2. Travel stitch down the right side of the small square until you reach the marked line; then work your way back across the block (bottom, green). Continue in the same manner until you have completed the block. This quilting option creates a secondary design and works best with matching thread so that the texture is the star, not the thread.

Use a Quilting Ruler

I didn't use a ruler to quilt the diagonal lines, but you may choose to use one if you prefer a more precise, less organic look.

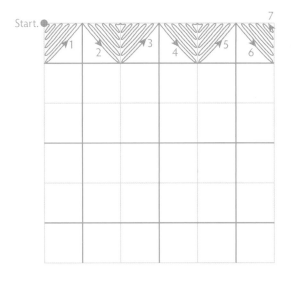

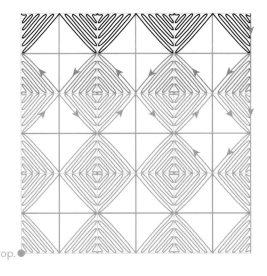

OPTION 6

1. Mark the center on each side of the block and draw an on-point square, drawing from mark to mark. Draw a second on-point square in the center of the block, using the corners of the center square as a guide. Draw both vertical and horizontal lines in the smaller on-point square (top, blue).

2. Stitching on the inside of the large on-point square, use a ruler to stitch ¼" from the marked line (top, green). Tie off. Stitch the large marked on-point square. Stitch feathers (page 14) in each block corner, making sure to stretch them into the corners (top, red).

3. Starting at a corner, use a ruler to stitch on the marked line of the small on-point square (center, green). Then stitch ribbon candy (page 15) between the stitched lines (center, red). Tie off.

4. Using a ruler and stitching on the inside of the small on-point square, stitch ¼" from the marked line. Stitch a continuous curved line around the inside of the stitched square two times. Then stitch a curved line from the corner of the stitched square to the center point and back to the next corner. Repeat in each center section. Stitch a second curved line in each section. Tie off.

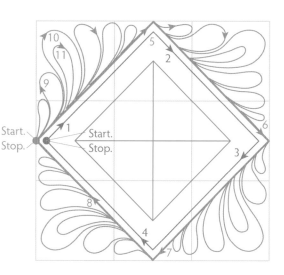

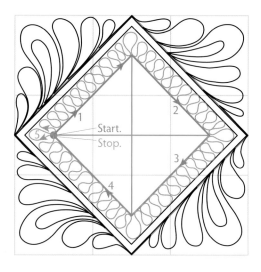

Snowball BLOCKS

Snowball blocks are incredibly fun to quilt.
I love to emphasize the ring shape when quilting
these blocks. There are so many ways to add
creative quilting to this simple patchwork block.

OPTION 1

1. Starting at the bottom corner of the top-left triangle, stitch a continuous curved line to the top-left corner and then to the top-right corner of the triangle. Echo stitch back to the starting point. Stitch a loop into the corner of the lower-right triangle, ending at the top-right corner (purple).

2. Stitch a slightly curved line down to the center point on the seamline in the top-middle square and then up to the next corner. Continue in the same way to work completely around the block (green).

3. When you reach the last square, stitch a slightly curved line to the center point on the seamline. Then stitch curved lines in the center square, making sure to touch the previously stitched lines (red). Stitch a curved line to the starting point.

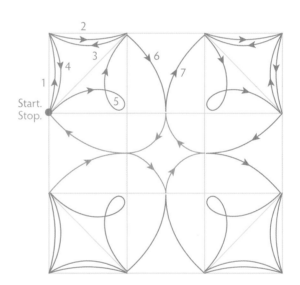

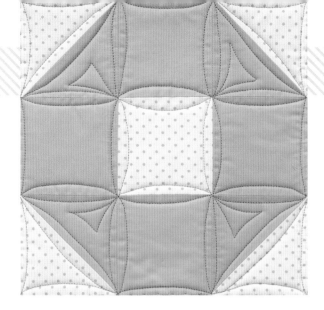

OPTION 2

1. Starting at the top-left corner, stitch a continuous curved line down the left side of the block to the first seamline. Stitch a curved line on each side of the diagonal seam. Stitch to the right and then add a small triangle in the 90° corner. Stitch a curved line up to the top of the block and back down on the opposite side of the seam (purple).

2. Following the green lines, stitch a curved line around each side of the center square. Stitch a curved line along the bottom of the top-middle square and then stitch up to the top of the block. Continue in the same way, working your way around the block in a clockwise direction. Don't stitch around the outside edges; you will stitch those on the way back.

3. Once the inside of the block is complete, follow the red lines to stitch in a counterclockwise direction to add curved lines along the outer edges.

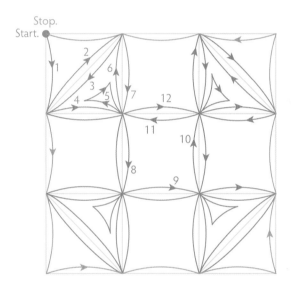

OPTION 3

1. Starting at the bottom corner of the top-left triangle, stitch ribbon candy toward the top-right corner of the triangle. (See "Ribbon Candy" on page 15.) Travel stitch to the corner of the top-right triangle and stitch ribbon candy in the triangle. In the same way, stitch ribbon candy in the lower-right and lower-left triangles (top).

2. Fill the area around the center square with swirls. (See "Swirls" on page 13.) When stitching the swirls, as soon as you reach a corner of the center square, stitch a double continuous curved line around the inside of the center square. Then finish stitching the swirls (bottom, red).

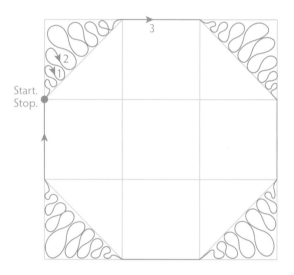

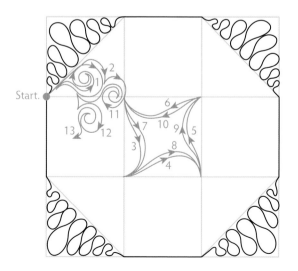

OPTION 4

1. Starting at the bottom corner of the top-left triangle, stitch a swirl that stretches into the corner and then stitch to the top-right corner of the triangle. Travel stitch to the corner of the top-right triangle and stitch a swirl in the same way. Continue around the block, stitching swirls in the lower-right and lower-left triangles (top, green). Tie off.

2. Fill the center square with pebbles (top, red). See "Pebbles" on page 14.

3. Starting at the lower-left corner of the center square, stitch a ring of feathers (page 14) around the center square (bottom, red). I didn't draw or quilt a spine for the feathers, but feel free to do so if it helps you stitch the feathers more easily.

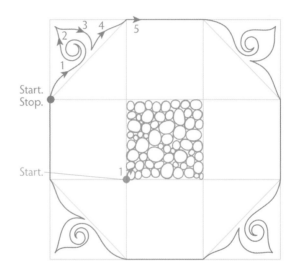

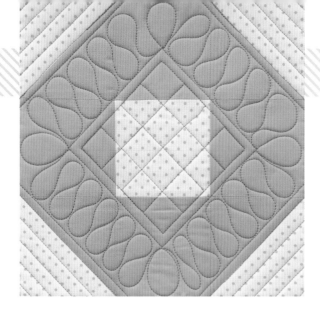

OPTION 5

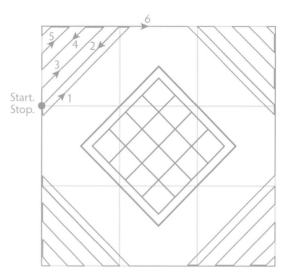

1. Draw an on-point square in the center of the block, using the corners of the center patchwork square as a guide. Draw a second square ¼" inside the first one. Draw a diagonal grid inside the smaller square. (My lines are spaced 1" apart; adapt the size of the grid to fit a larger or smaller block.)

2. Starting at the left side of the block, stitch a line ¼" inside the diagonal seamline (the line will be toward the center of the block). Stitch in the ditch along the seamline. Then stitch parallel diagonal lines in the top-left triangle, spacing them ½" apart. Travel stitch to the next corner. In the same way, stitch the top-right, lower-right, and lower-left corners of the block (top, in red). Tie off.

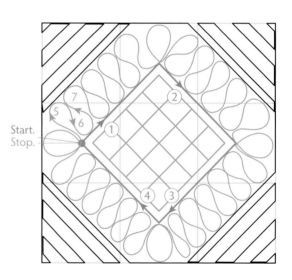

3. Starting at a corner, stitch on the drawn line for the large on-point square (center, in green). Stitch ribbon candy (page 15) between the two stitched lines (center, red). Tie off.

4. Using a ruler as a guide, stitch on the marked line for the small on-point square (bottom, green). Stitch on the marked grid lines (bottom, red).

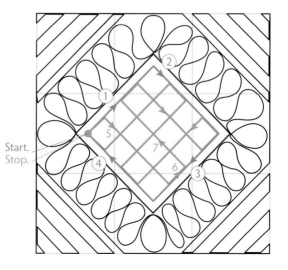

Churn Dash BLOCKS

The Churn Dash block is one of my all-time favorites. When quilting this block, I look for ways to highlight the shape of the Churn Dash to make it really stand out.

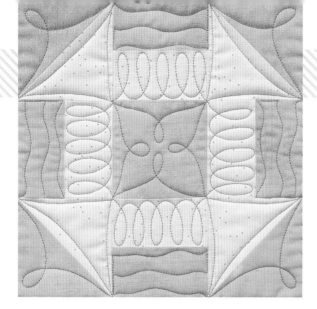

OPTION 1

1. Starting at the bottom corner of the top-left triangle, stitch a continuous curved line toward the top-left corner of the center square. Working around the block in a counterclockwise direction, stitch loops in the inner rectangle moving from top to bottom. When you reach the next triangle, stitch a continuous curved line around the inside of the triangle. Then stitch loops in the next inner rectangle moving from left to right. Continue in the same way to work around the block, pausing at the top-left corner of the center square (purple).

2. Stitch a slightly curved line into the center square, add a loop, and then stitch a curved line to the top-right corner of the square. Continue moving around the square in the same way (green).

3. When you reach the top-left corner of the center square, stitch into the top-left triangle; stitch a curved line along the last two sides of the triangle. You should be back at the starting point (green).

4. Working in a clockwise direction, stitch a loop that stretches into the corner of the top-left outer triangle. Stitch three wavy lines in the top rectangle to the right. Stitch in the ditch along the seamline to the top-left corner of the next triangle and stitch a loop. Continue, stitching a loop in outer triangles and wavy lines in outer rectangles (red).

Travel Stitching

When quilting the wavy lines, I stitched in the ditch to get to the next corner. It's much easier to travel stitch than to tie off and start again. If you are using matching thread, the stitches will practically disappear.

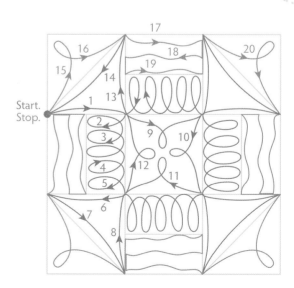

OPTION 2

1. Starting at the top-left corner of the center patchwork square, stitch horizontal lines back and forth in the inner rectangle. Be sure to stitch an odd number of lines so that you end up on the opposite side of the rectangle from where you started (green). Stitch in the ditch to the top-left corner of the inner triangle.

2. Stitch lines back and forth in the triangle, making the lines shorter as you move to the bottom corner of the triangle. Stitch the next inner rectangle in the same way as before, again using an odd number of lines. Continue stitching the inner rectangles and triangles until you reach the starting point (green).

3. Stitch matchstick lines on a diagonal through the center square (see "Matchstick Quilting," below right), moving from the top-left to the lower-right corner (red). Stitch in the ditch to the outside edge of the block.

4. Working in a clockwise direction, stitch diagonal matchstick lines in the outer triangle. Stitch an even number of vertical matchstick lines in the outer rectangle. Continue stitching the outer triangles and rectangles in the same way until you reach the stopping point.

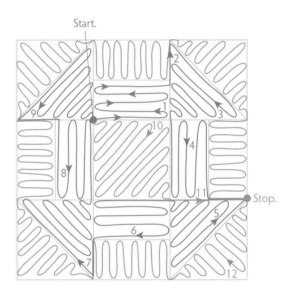

Matchstick Quilting

Matchstick quilting consists of straight, parallel lines of stitches that are spaced very close together to create a dense texture. On larger quilts, lines spaced 1" apart can have a matchstick look, and on smaller quilts, the spacing between lines can be as small as ⅛".

OPTION 3

1. Starting at the bottom corner of the top-left triangle, stitch ribbon candy in a clockwise direction around the block until you reach the starting point. (See "Ribbon Candy" on page 15.) Make the ribbon candy smaller in the narrow corners and stretch the design into the outer corner of each triangle (top, green).

2. Create a flower design in the top-left inner triangle by stitching a curved line, two big loops, and a curved line to the opposite corner of the triangle. I didn't mark any of the lines, but you can if it's easier for you. Stitch in the ditch down to the top-left corner of the center patchwork square. Stitch four humps in the inner rectangle, trying to make all the humps the same size. Continue stitching flowers and humps around the block until you get back to the top-left corner of the center square (top, red).

3. Stitch loops inside the humps, moving in a counterclockwise direction around the block (bottom, green). Using the previously stitched humps as a guide, stitch a crosshatch pattern of wavy lines in the center square (bottom, red).

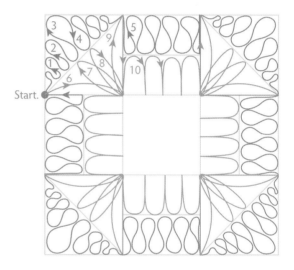

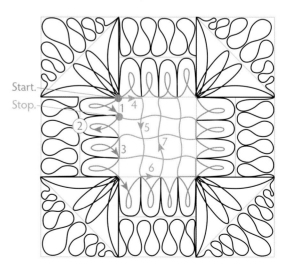

OPTION 4

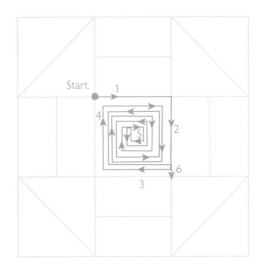

1. Starting at the top-left corner of the center patchwork square, stitch straight lines that spiral into the center of the square. Once you reach the center, stitch back out between the previously stitched lines (top).

2. Stitch a ring of feathers (page 14) around the center square, making sure to stretch them into the corners of the triangles to fill the space (center, red). Tie off, or travel in the ditch to the outside of the block.

3. Stitch straight lines that spiral into and back out of all the outer triangles and rectangles (bottom, red). Stitch in the ditch as needed to travel to the next triangle or rectangle.

Leave Space

When stitching spirals, leave space between the lines. For example, if you want lines spaced ¼" apart, leave ½" between the lines as you stitch into the center. As you stitch back out, you'll end up with lines ¼" apart.

OPTION 5

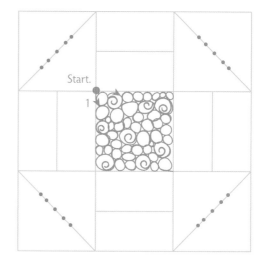

1. On the long side of each triangle, mark a dot at the center point. Measure ½" from the dot on one side and mark another dot. Measure ¼" from the second dot and mark a third dot. Repeat on the other side of each center dot (top, blue). These dots are guides for spacing; adjust as you wish.

2. Starting at the top-left corner of the center square, stitch pebbles (page 14) to fill the square (top, red). I randomly added swirls for extra texture. End at a corner of the square, or travel stitch to reach a corner.

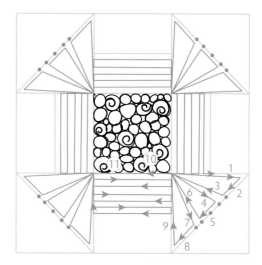

3. Working around the block in a clockwise direction, use a ruler to stitch a straight line that reaches from the 90° corner of the triangle to an adjacent corner. Stitch across the long side of the triangle until you reach a spacing dot. Then stitch back to the 90° corner. Repeat to stitch three small triangles inside the patchwork triangle (center, red).

4. Using a ruler, stitch five parallel straight lines in the inner rectangle. Stitch in the ditch to the next triangle. Continue in the same way to stitch all of the inner triangles and rectangles.

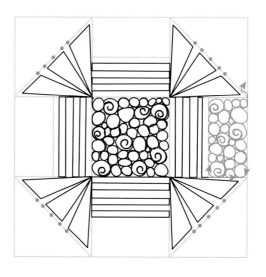

5. Stitch in the ditch to the outside edge of the block. Stitch pebbles to fill in the outer triangles and rectangles, travel stitching as needed (bottom, red).

Double X BLOCKS

The Double X block is the ideal block for grid quilting. All of the seamlines help break up the block into smaller sections without needing lots of marking.

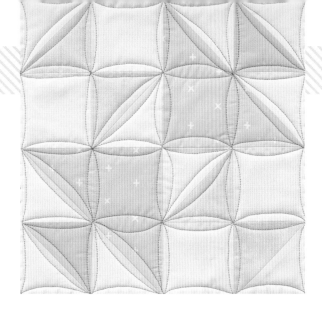

OPTION 1

1. Use the seams to mark guidelines that divide the large triangle into two small triangles and a square. (Or you can eyeball the guidelines as I did.)

2. Starting at the bottom-left corner of the block, stitch a continuous curved line upward until you reach the seamline. Stitch a curved line down one side of the diagonal seamline. Stitch a curved line on the other side of the diagonal seamline. Stitch a curved line on one side of the horizontal seamline and then on the other side of the seamline. Work your way from left to right and bottom to top, stitching curved lines on both sides of each seamline. Stitching in this order, you won't box yourself into a corner or forget to quilt a section (purple). When you reach a square, stitch the bottom, left, and top sides of the square only. When the left row is complete, stitch back to the bottom, adding a curved line to the right side of each patch (green).

3. Repeat the process to stitch rows 2, 3, and 4. When you reach the bottom of row 4, stitch along the right side of the row and then stitch curved lines in the patches on the bottom of the block until you reach the starting point (red).

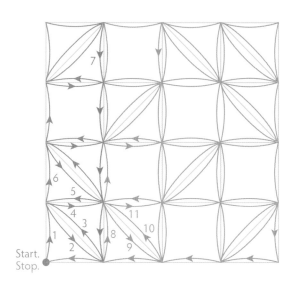

OPTION 2

1. This quilting design includes loops along the long edge of each triangle. Starting at the center of the block, follow the purple lines to stitch a continuous curved line toward the left, across the bottom of the small triangle. Stitch in a curved line on each side of the vertical seamline. Stitch a curved line across the bottom and up the left side of the square. Stitch a curved line across the top of the square, stopping at the corner.

2. Stitch on the other side of the horizontal seamline. Stitch a curved line up the left side and across the top of the outer triangle. Stitch a curved line on both sides of the diagonal seamline, adding a loop in the center of each line.

3. Stitch a curved line on each side of the vertical seamline. Stitch a curved line across the top and down the right side of the square. Stitch a curved line on each side of the horizontal seamline.

4. Stitch a curved line on each side of the diagonal seamline, adding a loop in the center of each line. Stitch a curved line along the right side of the triangle back to the starting point.

5. Following the green lines, stitch a curved line up the edge of the large triangle to the outer corner. Stitch a curved line across the top of the small triangle. Stitch a curved line on each side of the vertical seamline.

6. Stitch a curved line across the top and down the right side of the next small triangle. Stitch a curved line on each side of the diagonal seamline, adding a loop in the center of each line.

7. Stitch a curved line on each side of the horizontal seamline. Stitch a curved line down the right side of the small triangle. Along the diagonal seamline, stitch a curved line in each small triangle, adding a loop in the center of each line.

8. Stitch a curved line with a loop along the diagonal seamline of the large triangle. Stitch a curved line along the bottom of the large triangle back to the starting point.

9. Repeat the steps to stitch the remaining two quadrants in the same way, following the red lines.

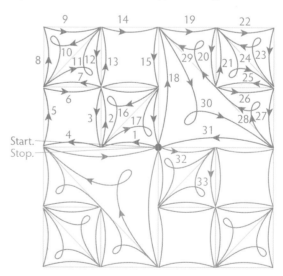

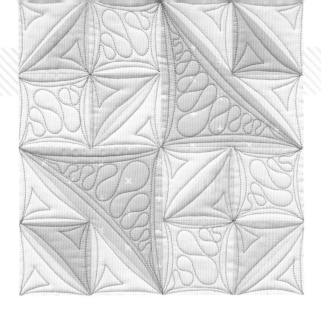

OPTION 3

1. Starting at the lower-right corner of a large triangle, stitch a double continuous curved lines inside the triangle (top, in green). Inside the curved lines, stitch ribbon candy (page 15) to the opposite corner (top, red).

2. Starting at the top-left corner of the small triangle, stitch a curved line along the diagonal seamline of each small triangle. Stitch along the bottom of the triangle. Stitch a small triangle shape in the 90° corner. Stitch a curved line on each side of the vertical seamline (bottom, green).

3. Follow the red lines to stitch a curved line on each side of the diagonal seamline. Stitch along the bottom and left side of the next triangle, adding a small triangle shape in the 90° corner. Stitch a curved line on one side of the horizontal seamline, stitch a small triangle shape in the 90° corner, and then stitch a curved line on the other side of the horizontal seamline. Stitch a curved line on the left side of the triangle. Do not tie off.

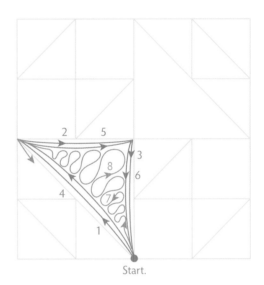

Start.

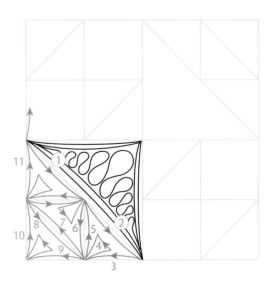

4. Starting at the lower-left corner of the upper-left quadrant, stitch a double continuous curved line inside the square. Stitch ribbon candy inside the curved lines, stitching from the lower-left to top-right corner of the square (purple).

5. Starting at the 90° corner of the top-inner triangle, stitch a curved line toward the left. Stitch a curved line on each side of the diagonal seamline. Stitch a curved line up the left side and across the top of the outer triangle, adding a small triangle shape in the 90° corner (green).

6. Stitch down the right side of the inner triangle and stitch a small triangle shape in the 90° corner. In the same way, stitch curved lines and small triangle shapes in the other two triangles before stitching the second square (red).

7. Stitch double curved lines and ribbon candy inside the second square, stopping in the top-right corner (red). Do not tie off.

8. Repeat step 1, stitching double curved lines and ribbon candy in the large triangle. Repeat steps 2–7 to stitch single curved lines and small triangle shapes in all the small triangles, as well as double curved lines and ribbon candy in the last two squares.

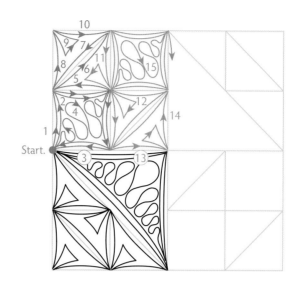

Practice Blocks

If you're not quite sure which design will work best for your quilt, make a practice block or two and try out the ideas before you commit. You may even try combining motifs in a new way.

OPTION 4

1. Draw a guideline to split the large triangle in half (or you can eyeball it as I did).

2. Starting at the top-left corner of the block, stitch double continuous curved lines around the small triangle unit. Stitch figure eights inside the curved lines to travel to the opposite corner (purple).

3. Stitch a curved line inside one square. Stitch a line with a loop in the center diagonally across the center of the square. Repeat to travel back to the center point. Repeat to stitch the other square (green).

4. Repeat step 2 to stitch the second triangle unit. You'll end in the center of the block (red). Do not tie off.

5. Starting at the center of the block, stitch feathers inside the large triangle. I stitched hook feathers, but you can use any form of feather you'd like. Start with a teardrop in the 90° corner of the triangle. Stitching one side at a time, stitch feathers that curl toward the teardrop. Stitch back down the spine to the teardrop. Stitch the other side of the feathers. After stitching the last feather, stitch in the ditch to the corner of a small triangle (green).

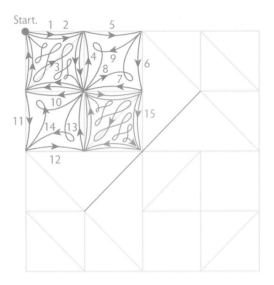

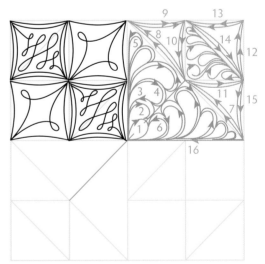

6. Stitch a curved line along the diagonal seamline in the first triangle. Stitch a double curved line around the inside of the next triangle. When you are back to the corner of the first triangle, stitch a curved line along the horizontal seamline. Stitch a double curved line around the inside of the third triangle. Stitch a feather in the fourth triangle. Stitch along the spine, back to the corner of the first triangle. Stitch a curved line down the right side of the first triangle and then stitch a second curved line around the inside the first triangle. You can tie off or stitch in the ditch to the center of the block (red, bottom of page 52).

7. Repeat step 5 to stitch hook feathers in the other large triangle (purple). Repeat step 6 to stitch double curved lines and a feather in the small triangles (green).

8. Repeat steps 2–4 to stitch the last quadrant, stopping in the bottom-right corner (red).

Hook Feathers

Hook feathers are magical because they eliminate backtracking. Each plume is quilted and then echoed on the way back to the spine. This technique is great for beginners, since backtracking can be hard to execute well.

OPTION 5

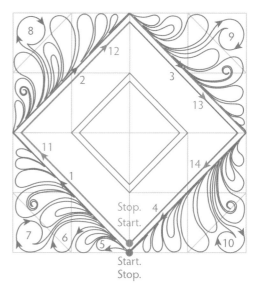

1. Draw four on-point squares: (1) in the center of the block using the diagonal seamline of the small triangles as a guide; (2) ¼" inside the first square; (3) using the diagonal seamline of the large triangles as a guide; (4) ¼" inside the large on-point square (all shown in blue).

2. Starting at the bottom center, stitch the marked large square. Then stitch feathers (page 14) that swirl around the outside of the block and fill in the corners (top, green). Tie off.

3. Stitch the second on-point square; tie off. Stitch the third on-point square. Stitch five small humps along each side and add a loop in the corners. Try to make all the humps the same size (center, green). Stitch a loop in each hump and corner loop (center, red). Tie off.

4. Stitch the smallest marked square (bottom, green). Stitch a curved line toward the center. Stitch a small loop that touches the side of the on-point square. Stitch curved lines on both sides of the seamline to make a larger loop. Continue stitching loops around the inside of the stitched square. After stitching the fourth small loop, stitch a curved line back to the starting point (red). Tie off.

Bear's Paw BLOCKS

Some of the options for this block require a bit of travel stitching in the seamlines. I prefer traveling rather than stopping and starting when possible. Remember, if you use matching thread, the stitching blends right in.

OPTION 1

1. Starting at the lower-left corner of the top-left paw unit, stitch a continuous curved line along the bottom of the triangle. Stitch a curved line around the inside of the large square (top, purple). Stitch curved lines on both sides of the diagonal seamline. Stitch a curved line along the right side of the triangle. Stitch curved lines on both sides of the horizontal seamline. Continue in the same way until you reach the corner square (top, green).

2. Stitch a curved line up the right side of the corner square, and continue stitching the small triangles along the top edge of the units as before (top, green). When you reach the top-right corner of the unit, stitch curved lines in each patch along the outer edge until you are back to the starting point (top, red).

3. Travel stitch about ¼" and stitch a horizontal wavy line to the opposite side of the block. Travel stitch up to the top-right paw unit and stitch the unit in the same way as the first (bottom, purple).

4. Travel stitch down to the approximate center of the rectangle and stitch a horizontal wavy line back to the left. Stitch one more wavy line to the right (bottom, green).

5. Travel stitch down to the lower-right paw unit. Stitch the unit in the same way as before. Travel stitch around the outside edge of the unit until you reach the vertical rectangle. Stitch a wavy line from the bottom to the top. Stitch a second wavy line back to the bottom (bottom, green).

6. Travel stitch to the left. Stitch the lower-left paw unit. Travel stitch about ¼" and stitch a wavy line back to the top (bottom, pink).

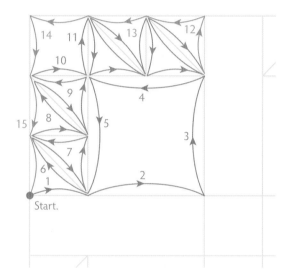

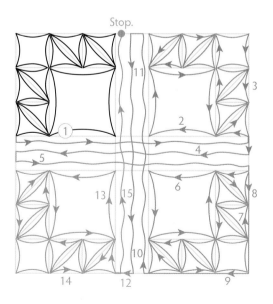

OPTION 2

1. Starting at the top-right corner of the top-left paw unit, stitch a curved line down the right side of the triangle. Stitch a loop in each triangle, moving to the left and then down (top, purple).

2. Stitch in the ditch to the center of the large square. Stitch a wavy line to the top of the square. Stitch in the ditch to the left and then down. Stitch a wavy line from left to right, and then stitch in the ditch to the starting point (top, purple).

3. Stitch curved lines along the seamlines in the triangles and corner square. When you reach the lower-left corner of the large square, stitch a curved line to the outer edge (top, green). Then stitch curved lines in each patch along the outer edge until you reach the starting point (top, red).

4. Travel stitch about ¼" along the outer edge of the block. Stitch four wavy lines in the vertical rectangle (top, red). Travel stitch ¼" to the top-left corner of the next paw unit, and stitch the unit in the same way as the first one.

5. Stitch in the ditch along the left seamline to the lower-left corner of the unit. Stitch curved lines inside the center square (bottom, green). Stitch in the ditch along the bottom seamline to reach the lower-right corner of the second unit.

6. Travel stitch about ¼" along the outer edge of the block. Stitch four wavy lines in the horizontal rectangle (bottom, green). Stitch the paw unit as before. Stitch in the ditch across the top and down the left side of the unit (bottom, red).

7. Travel stitch about ¼" along the outer edge of the block. Stitch four wavy lines in the vertical rectangle (bottom, red). Stitch the paw unit as before. Stitch in the ditch up the right side and across the top of the unit. Travel stitch about ¼" along the outer edge of the block. Stitch four wavy lines in the horizontal rectangle (bottom, red).

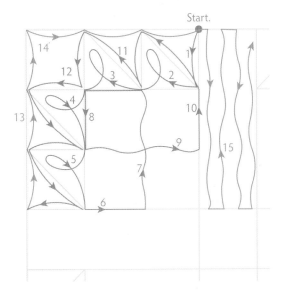

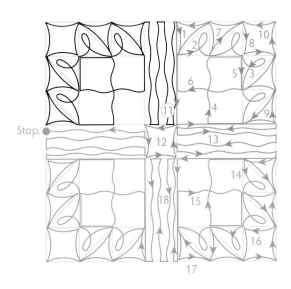

OPTION 3

1. Draw horizontal and vertical lines through the center of each large square to create four small squares. Starting at the top-left paw unit, stitch a curved triangle in the top-right outer triangle.

2. Travel stitch along the outer edge to the next triangle and stitch a curved triangle. At the 90° corner of the outer triangle, stitch a double curved line along two sides of the inner triangle. Travel stitch along the outer edge of the triangle to the corner square (red).

3. Stitch a curved triangle in one corner of the corner square, and then stitch double curved lines in the inner triangle. Travel stitch around the outer edges of the corner triangle and stitch a curved triangle in the opposite corner. Continue in the same way until you reach the lower-left corner of the unit (red).

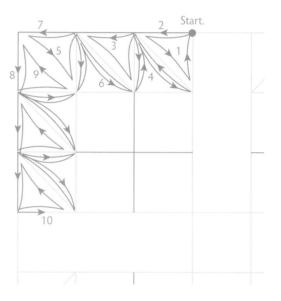

4. Stitch in the ditch until you reach the marked vertical line. Stitch double curved lines inside the first marked square. Stitch a swirl diagonally across the center of the small square. Repeat to stitch each small square (top, green).

5. Stitch in the ditch to the right and then up to the starting point. Travel stitch along the outer edge to the center point of the rectangle. Stitch elongated figure eights toward the center square, aiming for the center point along the seamline (top, red).

6. Stitch a curved line across the corner of the square, again aiming for the center point along the seamline. Stitch elongated figure eights toward the outer edge of the block (top, red).

7. Stitching back toward the center, add smaller figure eights between the larger ones. Stitch a curved line to the next side of the center square (bottom, purple). Stitch two lines of figure eights in the next rectangle in the same way as before (bottom, purple and green).

8. Repeat to stitch the fourth rectangle in the same way. Stitch a curved line across the last corner of the center square (bottom, green). Stitch small figure eights between the large ones in the first rectangle (bottom, red).

9. To stitch the top-right paw, travel stitch along the outer edge to the lower-right corner of the unit. Stitch the second paw unit exactly the same as the first one (bottom, red). Repeat to stitch the third and fourth units, travel stitching along the outer edge as you move around the block.

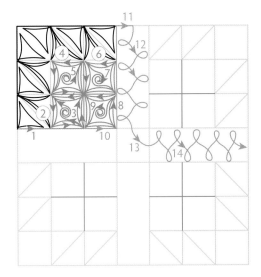

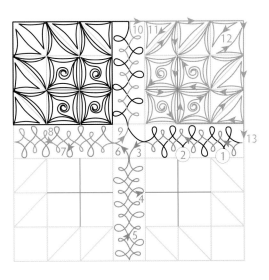

corner of the paw unit. Stitch double curved lines in the center square (center, green).

6. Stitch in the ditch to the starting point for the next paw unit. Continue in the same way to work completely around the block (bottom).

OPTION 4

1. Draw an on-point square in the center of each large square. Starting at the corner of a marked square, stitch double continuous curved lines inside the marked square (top, purple). Stitch figure eights to travel to the other side of the on-point square (top, purple).

2. Stitch a double curved line in the top-right corner of the large square. Stitch a single curved line along the outside edge of the on-point square. Repeat in each corner of the square (top, green).

3. Stitch in the ditch to the top-right corner of the large square. Stitch a double curved line along the diagonal seamline. Stitch a single curved line along the bottom of the triangle. Stitch a double curved line along the straight seamline. Repeat to stitch the three remaining inner triangles (top, red).

4. Stitch in the ditch to reach the outer edge of the block. Stitch lines back and forth in the outer triangles. Stitch back-and-forth diagonal lines in the corner square (center, purple). See "Matchstick Quilting" on page 43.

5. When you reach the top-right corner of the paw unit, travel stitch into the rectangle and stitch swirls toward the center square, ending at the

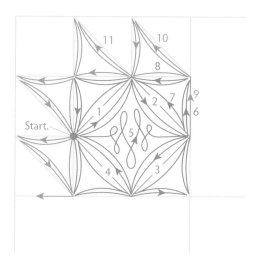

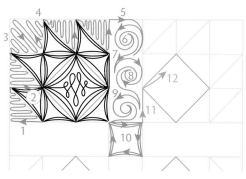

OPTION 5

1. Using two adjacent diagonal seams as guidelines, draw two lines into each rectangle with the 90° corner of the intersecting lines pointing toward the center of the block (blue). Using a ruler, stitch along the diagonal seamlines and onto the marked line. Stitch ribbon candy (page 15) in this triangle (top, purple).

2. In the next outer triangle, stitch a continuous curved line down the straight seamline and along the diagonal seamline to the outer edge. Stitch a double curved line along the outer edge to the corner of the outer square. Stitch a double curved line in the outer square. Stitch a swirl diagonally across the square to reach the opposite corner (top, green).

3. Repeat steps 1 and 2 to stitch around the outer edges of the block. Tie off.

4. Starting at the lower-left corner of the large square in the top-left paw unit, use a ruler to stitch an angled line toward the top-left corner and over to the top-right corner of the square. Stitch a second angled line back to where you started to make a diamond shape. Stitch a third and then fourth line to make a smaller diamond inside the first one. Stitch a feather inside the smaller diamond (top, red).

5. Stitch in the ditch around each inner triangle. Echo stitch an additional triangle about ¼" inside the previously stitched line (bottom, purple).

6. Stitch in the ditch to the top-left corner of the center square. Stitch a double curved line in the center square. Travel stitch ¼" to the right. Using a ruler, stitch parallel straight lines inside the vertical rectangle, moving from left to right and spacing the lines approximately ¼" apart. Stitch in the ditch to the top-left corner of the next paw unit (bottom, purple).

7. Repeat steps 4–6 to stitch each paw unit and the rectangles (bottom).

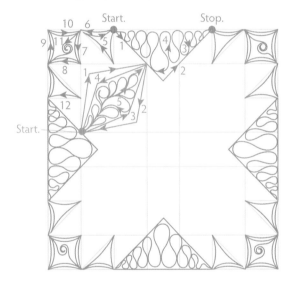

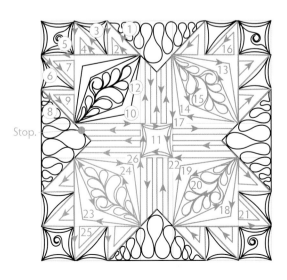

Granny Square BLOCKS

Traditionally known as Grandmother's Pride or Nine Patch Checkerboard, this block is often called *Granny Square* by quilters today because it reminds them of the crocheted afghans called granny squares. Whatever you call it, the piecing in this block provides the perfect grid for quilting. Practice your continuous curves—they will definitely come in handy for these blocks!

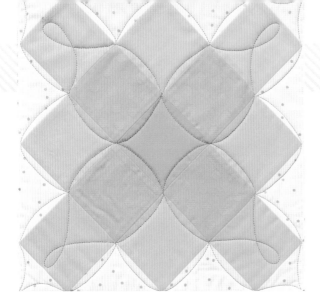

OPTION 1

1. Starting at the top-left corner of the block, stitch a continuous curved line down to the left corner of the top-left square. Stitch a curved line toward the bottom corner of the square (green).

2. Stitch a big loop in the top square that stretches to the other side. Stitch a curved line toward the bottom corner of the second square. Stitch curved lines inside the center square. Then stitch up to the other side of the second square (green).

3. Stitch a big loop in the top-right square, ending at the bottom of the square. Continue stitching around the block in the same way until you reach the bottom of the top-left square (green).

4. Working in a counterclockwise direction, stitch two curved lines in each of the outer triangles until you are back to the starting point (red).

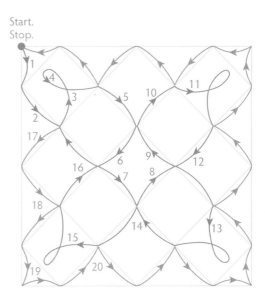

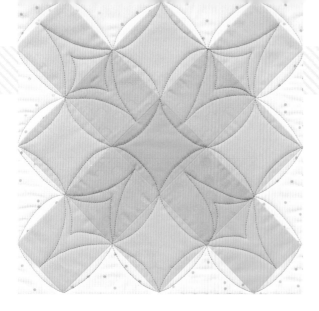

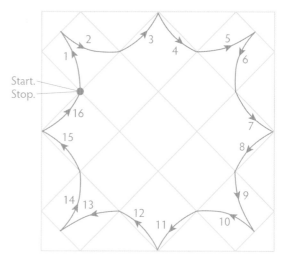

OPTION 2

1. Starting at the bottom corner of the top-left patchwork, stitch a slightly curved line to the center point on the seamline and then back down to the opposite corner. In the next square, stitch a curved line up to the top corner and then down to the other side. Repeat, moving around the outer squares in a clockwise direction until you reach the starting point (top).

2. Moving in a counterclockwise direction, stitch a curved line down toward the center square. Stitch curved lines in the center square. Stitch a curved line to the bottom of the outer square (center, red).

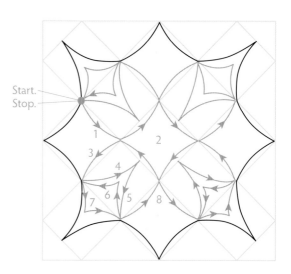

3. Stitch a slightly curved line to the center point on the seamline and then back down to the opposite corner. Stitch two angled lines to create a small diamond shape. Repeat, moving around the squares in the same direction until you reach the starting point (center, red).

4. Moving in a counterclockwise direction, stitch a curved line all around the outer edges of the squares (bottom, red).

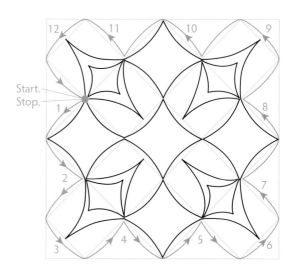

OPTION 3

1. Draw two diagonal lines through the center square to create four small on-point squares. Refer to "Option 2" on page 64 to stitch curved lines in all of the squares except the center square (top, purple and green). In the center square, use the marked lines to stitch a double curved line inside each of the small on-point squares (top, red).

2. From the starting point, work in a clockwise direction to stitch ribbon candy (page 15) in the small diamond shape. In the next square, stitch a second curved line inside the first one and then stitch ribbon candy across the square to travel to the opposite corner. Continue in the same way until you reach the starting point (bottom, green). Stop and tie off.

3. Around the outer edges of the squares and working in a counterclockwise direction, stitch a single curved line in the corner triangle. In the next triangle, stitch curved lines and a loop to travel to the top of the triangle. Then stitch a second double curved line in the same triangle. Stitch each triangle around the perimeter in the same way. When you reach the triangle where you started, stitch a double curved line and loop back to the starting point (bottom, red).

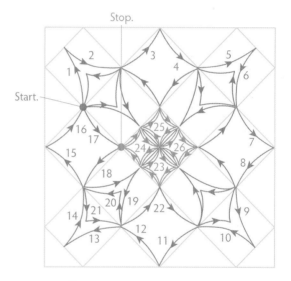

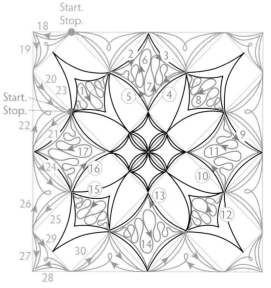

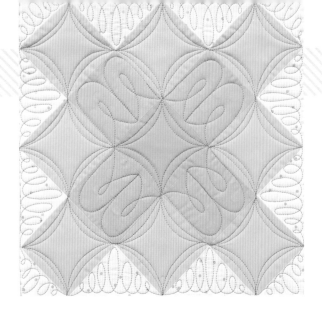

OPTION 4

1. Starting at the center on the left side and working in a counterclockwise direction, stitch loops in the triangles around the outside edges of the block until you reach the starting point. Make sure to adjust the size of the loops to fill the triangles (top, purple).

2. In the outer ring of squares, stitch a continuous curved line along the outermost edge of each square (top, green). Working in a clockwise direction, stitch a second curved line in each square (top, red). At the top of the bottom-left square, stitch a curved line around the inside of each square, working in a counterclockwise direction.

3. At the right corner of the middle square, stitch a double curved line in the center square (bottom, purple).

4. Stitch two humps in each of the squares forming the middle ring (bottom, green). Then stitch a loop in each hump. When you are back to the right corner of the center square, continue echo stitching a second curved line in the remaining squares of the outer ring. Stitch curved lines back to the starting point.

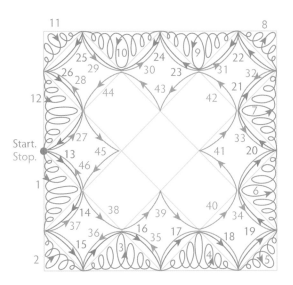

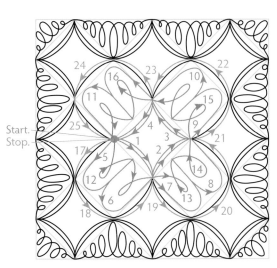

OPTION 5

1. Starting at the bottom-left corner of the top-left square, use a ruler to stitch in the ditch along the seamline. When you reach the top-middle square, stitch across the center to the opposite side. Stitch in the ditch of the next square. Continue in this way to create an octagon shape around the ring of middle squares (top, purple). Tie off.

2. Using a ruler, stitch a line ¼" outside of the previously stitched line (top, green). Stitch swirls on the outside of the stitched line, filling the entire outer area of the block (top, red). Tie off.

3. Stitch a small circle in the middle of the center square. Stitch a spiral inside the circle (bottom, green). Stitch 10 or 11 little humps around the outside of the circle. Stitch five curved petals around the circle and echo stitch each petal. (If you have 10 hills, each petal should contain two hills.) Stitch five large petals and echo stitch each petal. Echo stitch around the flower until you fill the space (bottom, red).

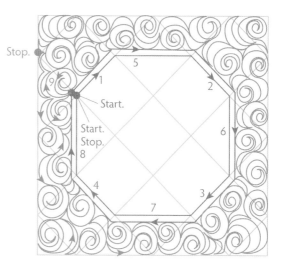

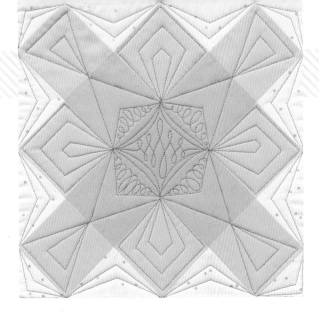

OPTION 6

1. Starting at the left corner of the top-left square and working in a clockwise direction, use a ruler to quilt a straight line stopping about ½" from the 90° corner of the triangle. Pivot, and then stitch to the top of the square. Continue to stitch all the triangles around the outer edges of the block in the same way (green).

2. Working in a counterclockwise direction, stitch a second line about ½" from the previously stitched line. You can mark the lines if you want exact measurements, but I love organic quilting so I didn't mark anything (red). Tie off.

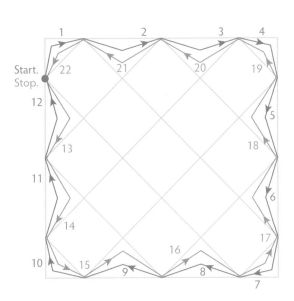

Ruler Work

When using rulers, it's helpful to add nonslip ruler grips. This eliminates any slippage of the ruler that can result in wobbly lines.

3. Starting at the left corner of the center square, use a ruler to quilt a diagonal line that ends about ¼" from the top corner of the top-left outer square. Stitch across the top-left edge of square. Then stitch toward the top corner of the center square, stopping where the previously stitched line crosses the seamline at the lower-right edge (top, red).

4. Stitch a small triangle inside the top-left square and then finish stitching the straight line to the top corner of the center square (top, red).

5. Echo stitch the shape of the top-middle square. Stitch two shapes inside the stitched square; each shape will be slightly different (top, red).

6. Repeat steps 3–5, working around the block in a clockwise direction until you reach the starting point.

7. Use a ruler to stitch a triangle in the top-left inner square, with the corner of the triangle about 1" from the center square. Stitch a triangle on each side of the center square. Stitch loops inside each of the triangles (bottom, green).

8. Stitch a double continuous curved line in the center square. Stitch figure eights across the center of the square (bottom, red). Stop and tie off.

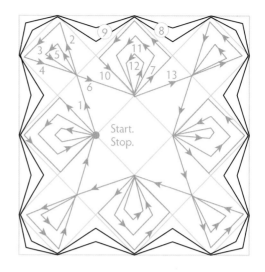

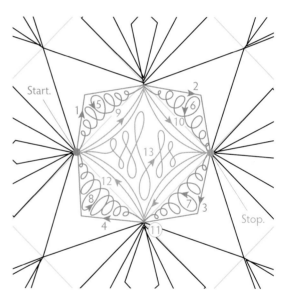

Friendship Star BLOCKS

**Friendship Stars are fun to quilt.
From easy to more challenging, the quilting design
you choose can really make the stars pop!**

OPTION 1

1. Starting at the lower-right corner of the top-left square, stitch a wavy continuous line around the inside of the square. Echo stitch a second wavy line inside the square (purple).

2. Stitch a wavy line around the inside of the star-point triangle.

3. Stitch a wavy line across the top of the center square. Stitch a wavy line inside the top-outer triangle (green).

4. Repeat step 1 to stitch two wavy lines in the top-right square (green).

5. Stitch a wavy line down the right side of the center square. Stitch wavy lines in both triangles and in the lower-right square. Continue in the same way until you reach the starting point (red).

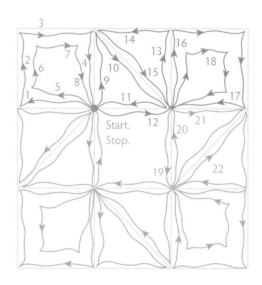

Make It Wavy

Wavy lines are the best thing ever! No one will know or care if the lines aren't perfectly straight.

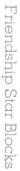

OPTION 2

1. Starting at the tip of the top star-point triangle, stitch a continuous curved line down the left side of the triangle. Stitch along the diagonal seamline and bottom of the left star-point triangle. In the same way, stitch two sides of the bottom and right star-point triangles (top, purple).

2. When you reach the last 90° corner, stitch a curved line down the left side of the triangle. Working in a clockwise direction, stitch a curved line along the remaining side of each triangle (top, green).

3. Stitch a curved line along each side of the center square, working in a counterclockwise direction. Then stitch a curved line along the diagonal seamline of the top star-point triangle back to the starting point (top, red).

4. Working in a clockwise direction, stitch a curved line along the diagonal seamline and each side of the vertical seamline. In the corner square, stitch a large loop or petal that extends toward the outer corner. Stitch a curved line along the horizontal seamline (bottom, green).

5. Repeat step 4 to stitch curved lines around the outer edges of the star and add a large loop in each corner square (bottom, red).

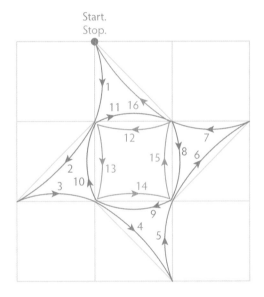

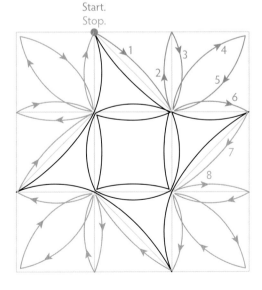

OPTION 3

1. Starting at the tip of the top star-point triangle, stitch a continuous curved line toward the top-right corner of the outer triangle. Stitch to the lower-right corner of the same triangle. Stitch two curved lines back to where you started to create double curved lines (top, green).

2. Stitch ribbon candy across the star-point triangle, working from the outer tip toward the lower-right corner. (See "Ribbon Candy" on page 15.) Stitch in the ditch to the outer tip of the next star-point triangle (top, red).

3. Stitch a single curved line along each short sides of the outer triangle. Then stitch curved lines back to the point. Stitch ribbon candy across the triangle. Repeat to stitch the bottom and left triangles (top, red).

4. Stitch a double curved line in the center square. Stitch in the ditch back to the starting point (bottom, green).

5. Travel stitch across the top of the outer triangle to the top-right corner square. Stitch a double curved line in the square. Stitch a swirl diagonally across the inside of the square to the lower-right corner (bottom, red).

6. Travel stitch across the outer triangle to the top-right corner of the next square. Repeat step 5 to stitch the three remaining squares (bottom, red).

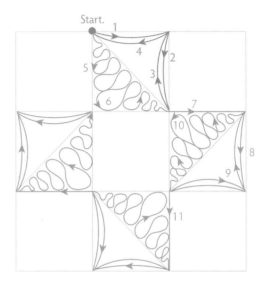

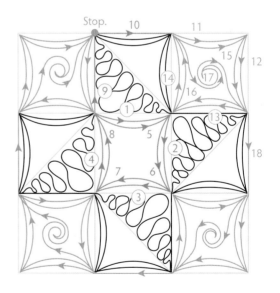

OPTION 4

1. Visually divide the center square diagonally to create four quarter-square triangles. I didn't mark the square, but you can if you wish. Starting in the middle of the center square, stitch a straight line toward the top-right corner of the square. Then stitch toward the tip of the right star-point triangle. Stitch along the diagonal seamline and back to the center of the square. Echo stitch inside the previously stitched line. Repeat to stitch the bottom section of the star. Then stitch the left and top sections (green). Tie off.

2. Starting along one side, stitch swirls in the outer triangles and squares, travel stitching to the next area as needed to fill in around the star (red).

Switch It Up!

Are you tired of swirls? Switch it up and stitch pebbles around the star instead. Any background fill will work, so have fun with it.

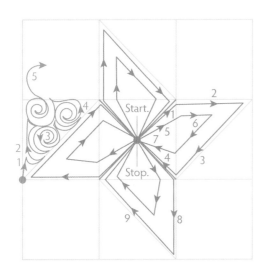

OPTION 5

1. Starting at the tip of the top star-point triangle, stitch feathers (see "Feathers" on page 14) across the corner square and outer triangle until you reach the tip of the next triangle. Add a swirl plume that reaches into the outer corner of the square. Continue in the same way until you reach the starting point (top, red).

2. Using a ruler, stitch grid lines spaced about ½" apart inside of the star. I didn't measure or mark the lines, but you can if you want to be precise. I did use the marks on my ruler to approximate the ½" spacing. Stitch all of the vertical lines first, and then stitch in the ditch to the outer tip of the left triangle (bottom, green). Use a ruler to stitch the horizontal lines (bottom, red).

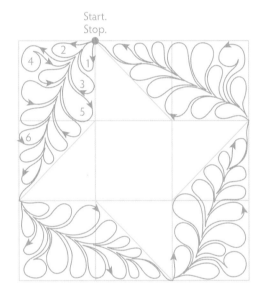

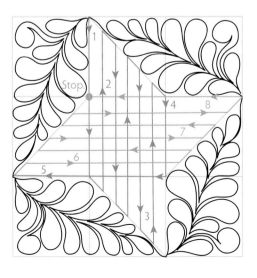

OPTION 6

1. Draw a line to divide each corner square diagonally. Using the diagonal seamlines as a guide, draw lines to divide the star-point triangles in half. Draw two diagonal lines in the center square to create four quarter-square triangles.

2. Starting at the top-right corner of the top-left square, stitch along the marked diagonal line. Create a spiraling triangle by stitching along each side of the triangle until you reach the center, and then spiral back out (top, green). When you return to where you started, stitch ribbon candy that stretches to the next corner. (See "Ribbon Candy" on page 15.) Repeat until you are back to the starting point (top, red).

3. Stitch spiraling triangles in each of the smaller marked triangles (bottom, green). Travel stitch as needed to move to the next triangle (bottom, red). Remember, with matching thread you will see the texture, not the thread.

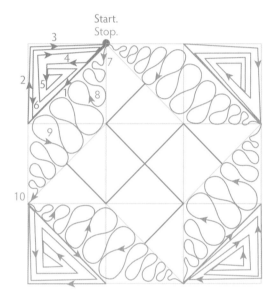

Sawtooth Star BLOCKS

The Sawtooth Star block offers many variations
for quilting. You can break up the star
center into smaller sections or quilt it as
one large center. "Fancy up" the star points
or keep them simple. Just have fun!

4. Working in a clockwise direction, stitch a loop in the center of the outer triangle. When you reach the top-right square, stitch slightly curved lines along the top and right sides. Continue stitching the outer triangles and squares in the same way until you reach the starting point (bottom, red).

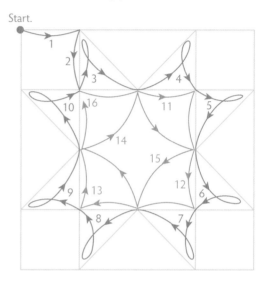

OPTION 1

1. Starting at the top-left corner of the block, stitch a curved line toward the triangle point. Stitch a curved line down to the lower-right corner of the square. Working in a clockwise direction, stitch a loop up into the point of each star-point triangle (top, green).

2. When you reach the top-left corner of the center square, stitch two curved lines along the top of the square, using the seam intersections as a guide. In the same way, stitch two curved lines along the right side and bottom of the center square. On the left side, stitch one curved line. Then stitch a curved line from one seam intersection to the next around the inside of the square. Stitch a second curved line on the left side of the square to reach the top-left corner of the center square (top, red).

3. In the corner square, stitch a curved line to the left. Working in a counterclockwise direction, stitch curved lines along both diagonal seamlines. Then stitch curved lines along the top and right side of the next corner square. Continue in the same way until you reach the tip of the top-left triangle (bottom, green).

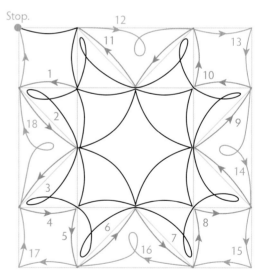

in the ditch down to the lower-right corner and then stitch about halfway across the side of the next triangle. Stitch a wavy line to the top of the square. Then stitch in the ditch to the center of the square and stitch a wavy line down to the bottom of the square. Continue until you have three wavy lines in each direction (bottom, green).

5. Stitch in the ditch all the way around the center square until you reach the center point on the left side of the square. Stitch a curved line to the outer tip of the triangle (bottom, red).

OPTION 2

1. Starting at the lower-left corner of the top-left square and working in a clockwise direction, stitch a loopy line to the diagonally opposite corner of the square. Think of making a large letter L with a loop at both the top and bottom (top, green).

2. Stitch loops across the outer triangle, adjusting the size of the loops to fill the triangle. Continue in the same way, alternating the designs, until you reach the starting point (top, green).

3. Working in a clockwise direction, stitch a curved line from the triangle tip to the top-left corner of the center square. Stitch a curved line up to the tip of the triangle and back down along the diagonal seamline. In the next triangle, stitch a curved line along the diagonal seamline to the tip and back down to the top-right corner of the center square. Repeat to stitch the triangles on the right side and bottom of the block. On the left side of the block, stitch two sides of the first triangle in the same way as before (top, red).

4. Stitch in the ditch until you're about halfway down the side of the triangle. Stitch a wavy line across the center square to the right side. Stitch

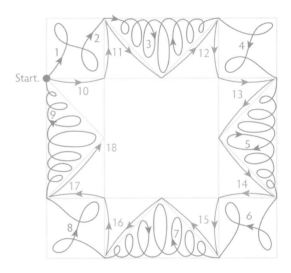

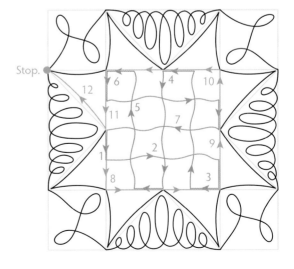

5. Working in a counterclockwise direction, echo stitch a second curved line along each curved line in the outer triangle to reach the lower-left square. Stitch a curved line toward the bottom-left corner and then the bottom-right corner. Echo stitch up the right side and across the top. Then echo stitch down the left side and across the bottom of the square to create double curved lines (bottom, red). Continue stitching all of the outer triangles and corner squares in the same way until you are back to where you started.

OPTION 3

1. Starting at the lower-left corner of the top-left square, stitch a continuous curved line along the bottom and right side of the square. Stitch a curved line along the diagonal seamline of the large triangle. Stitch feathers (page 14) inside each of the star-point triangles (top, green). Think of the long diagonal side of the small triangle as the feather spine. The feathers will curl into the point.

2. Travel stitch back down the spine of the second feather. Stitch a curved line along the diagonal seamline of the outer triangle (top, green).

3. Stitch a curved line on the left side and bottom of the next square. Continue in the same way around the block, making sure to stitch feathers in the star-point triangles as you go. When you reach the left side, stitch only the bottom star-point triangle (top, red).

4. Before stitching feathers in the last star-point triangle, stitch swirls in the center square. If you stitch yourself into a corner, tie off or stitch in the ditch back to the last star-point triangle. Stitch feathers in the star-point triangle. Stitch a curved line along the diagonal seamline of the outer triangle back to the starting point (bottom, green).

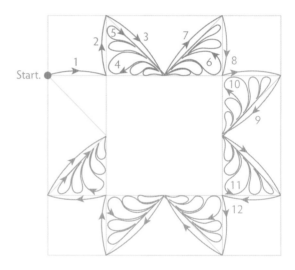

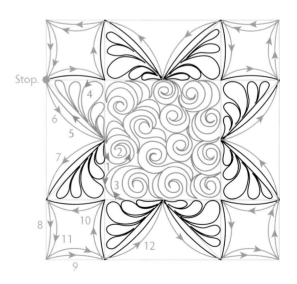

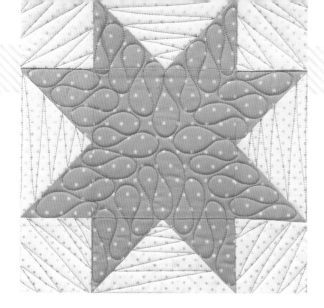

OPTION 4

1. Draw two diagonal lines through the center square to create four quarter-square triangles. Starting at the tip of the top-left star-point triangle, stitch ribbon candy that follows the V shape of the marked lines. (See "Ribbon Candy" on page 15.) When you reach the tip of the top-right triangle, stitch in the ditch down the side of the square and across the bottom to the tip of the next triangle. Continue stitching ribbon candy in all four sections (top).

2. After stitching ribbon candy in the last section, stitch in the ditch across the top of the star-point triangle as needed. Starting at the lower-right corner of the outer square, zigzag stitch straight lines across the square until you reach the top-left corner. Travel stitch along the outer edge until you reach the top-left corner of the next triangle. Zigzag stitch straight lines across the outer triangle. Stitch in the ditch along the diagonal seamline and down the left side of the top-right square. Zigzag stitch straight lines across the square. Continue in the same way to zigzag stitch the remaining triangles and squares (bottom).

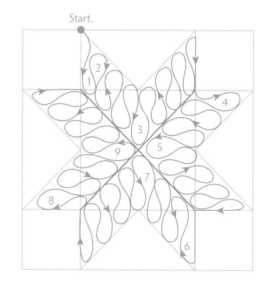

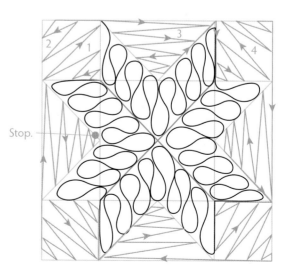

OPTION 5

1. Draw an on-point square in the middle of the center square (blue). Starting at the lower-left corner of the top-left square, stitch feathers diagonally across the square. Make sure to stretch the feathers to fill the corners, adding echo loops as desired (purple).

2. When you reach the top-outer triangle, stitch a one-sided feather that curls into the point of the triangle. The long side of the triangle will act as the spine of the feather. Add an echo loop inside feathers as desired. Continue working around the entire block to stitch feathers in each corner square and outer triangle (purple). Tie off.

3. Starting at the left corner of the marked square, stitch a curved line to the left along the diagonal seamline. Working in a clockwise direction, stitch a single curved line on two sides of each star-point triangle until you are back to the starting point (green). Repeat to echo stitch a second curved line on the same two sides of each star-point triangle (red).

4. Work in a clockwise direction to stitch a single curved line along the bottom of each star-point triangle. Repeat to echo stitch a second curved line (top, green). Stitch a curved line to the top-left corner of the center square and then stitch a curved line to the top corner of the marked square. In the same way, stitch all around the inside of the center square twice to create a double curved line (top, purple).

5. Stitch curved lines twice around the outer edge of the marked square (top, red). Stitch curved lines twice around the inner edge of the marked square (bottom, green). When you are back to the left side of the marked square, stitch figure eights across the center of the square (bottom, red). Stop on the right side of the square and tie off.

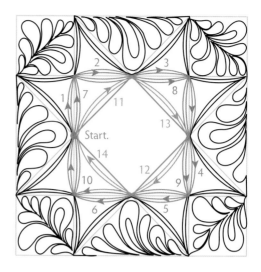

Balanced Feathers

Worried about keeping your feathers balanced in the corner squares? Draw a diagonal line from corner to corner to use as the spine.

Ohio Star BLOCKS

The Ohio Star block is another favorite because the star points create a triangle. The triangle grid gives many options for quilting without requiring a lot of marking.

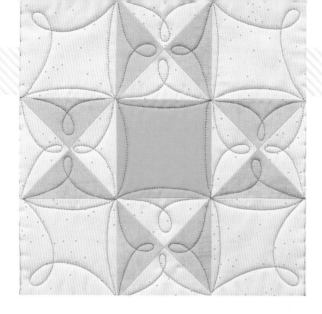

OPTION 1

1. Starting at the lower-left corner of the top-left square, stitch a loop that stretches diagonally across the square to the opposite corner. Stitch a continuous curved line down toward the lower-right corner of the square. Stitch a curved line around each side of the center square (purple).

2. Working in a clockwise direction, stitch loops inside the triangles adjacent to the center square (green).

3. Stitch a loop going upward in the top-left triangle. Stitch a loop in the top-outer triangle, and then stitch a loop going downward in the top-right triangle (red).

4. Stitch a curved line along the left side of the top-right square. Stitch a loop that stretches diagonally across the square. Stitch a curved line across the bottom of the square (red).

5. Repeat steps 3 and 4, moving around the block until you reach the starting point (red).

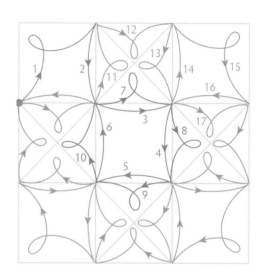

OPTION 2

1. Starting at the lower-right corner of the top-left square, stitch a continuous curved line to the left and then back to where you started. Stitch a curved line to the top and then back to where you started (purple).

2. Working in a clockwise direction, stitch a curved line on each short side of the top-left triangle. Stitch a curved line along each short side of the top-outer triangle. Stitch a curved line on each short side of the top-right triangle (purple).

3. Repeat steps 1 and 2, stitching double curved lines in each corner square and single curved lines in the triangles, until you reach the starting point (green).

4. Stitch curved lines around the inside of the center square. Stitch loops that stretch from the stitched line inside the center square (red).

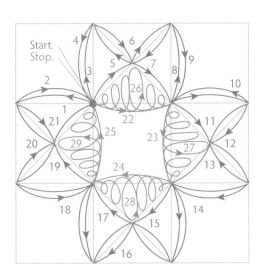

4. Using the marked lines as a guide, stitch feathers in each of the quarter-square triangles with the plumes curling toward the corners of the drawn lines. Use the seamline around the center square as the spine. Stitch in the ditch to move around the square until you are back at the starting point (bottom, red).

OPTION 3

1. Draw two diagonal lines through the center square to divide the square into four quarter-square triangles (blue). Starting at the lower-right corner of the top-left square, stitch a continuous curved line to the left and back to the starting point. Stitch a curved line to the top of the square. Stitch a curved line along each short side of the top-outer triangle. Echo stitch back along each curved line in the triangle. Echo stitch back to the starting point. Stitch a swirl that reaches into the corner of the square (top, purple). I stitched a pointy little hat on mine.

2. Stitch feathers in the triangles that are below and to the right of the corner square, using the longest side of each triangle as the spine of the feathers. After the feathers are stitched, stitch in the ditch down the spine to the starting point (top, green).

3. Stitch ribbon candy (page 15) in the triangle adjacent to the top of the center square (top, red). Continue stitching the corner squares and triangles in the same way until you reach the starting point.

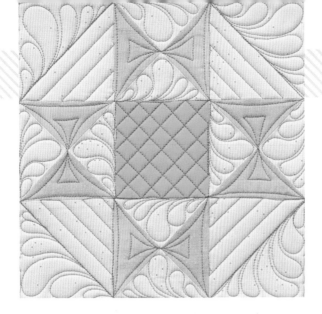

5. Stitch feathers in the triangle adjacent to the top of the center square, using the seamline as the spine. When you reach the other side of the center square, stitch curved lines and an echo triangle in the next star-point triangle in the same way as the first one (bottom, green).

OPTION 4

1. Draw a diagonal line across each of the corner squares. Starting at the lower-left corner of the top-left square and using the drawn line as the spine, stitch feathers (see "Feathers" on page 14) that stretch out toward the outer corner (top, green).

2. Stitch feathers in the top-outer triangle, using the long side of the triangle as the spine. Continue stitching the corner squares and outer triangles in the same way until you reach the starting point (top, red).

3. Stitch in the ditch about ½". Stitch parallel straight lines in the bottom half of the corner square, spacing them about ½" apart (bottom, purple).

4. When you reach the lower-right corner of the square, stitch a continuous curved line to the tip of the star-point triangle. Stitch a curved line down to the 90° corner, stitch a small echo triangle, and then stitch back to the bottom of the triangle (bottom, purple).

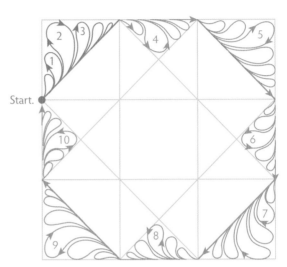

6. Stitch in the ditch about ½". Stitch straight lines in the bottom half of the corner square, working from the corner toward the feathers and spacing the lines about ½" apart. Stitch in the ditch along the bottom of the corner square until you reach the top-right corner of the center square (bottom, green on page 88).

7. Repeat steps 4–6, stitching the triangles in the same way until you are back to the top-left corner of the center square (bottom, red on page 88).

8. Stitch in the ditch down about ½". Stitch diagonal lines, working from the top-left to the lower-right corner of the square and spacing lines about ½" apart (green). Stitch in the ditch to the lower-left corner. Stitch diagonal lines from the lower-left corner to the top-right corner, spacing them about ½" apart (red). Tie off.

4. Stitch double curved lines around the inside of the top-right square. Stitch figure eights across the center of the square to travel to the opposite corner.

5. Repeat steps 3 and 4, working around the block in a clockwise direction.

OPTION 5

1. Draw horizontal and vertical lines in the center square to create four smaller squares (blue). Starting at the lower-left corner of the top-left square, stitch a continuous curved line (page 12) to the lower-right corner. Stitch double curved lines inside each of the smaller marked squares (top, purple and green). When you're back to the top-left corner of the center square, stitch a single curved line along each short side of the triangles adjacent to the center square (top, green).

2. When you're back to where you started, stitch a curved line up to the top-right corner of the corner square. Stitch to the top-left corner; then down to the lower-left corner of the square. Stitch curved lines around the square again for a double curved line. Stitch figure eights across the center of the square to travel to the opposite corner (top, red).

3. Starting at the tip of the top-left triangle, stitch ribbon candy (page 15) to the bottom tip. Echo stitch a curved line to the bottom tip of the top-right triangle. Stitch ribbon candy to the top tip of the triangle. Working to the left, stitch a curved line along each short side of the top-outer triangle and echo stitch back to the right to create a double curved line.

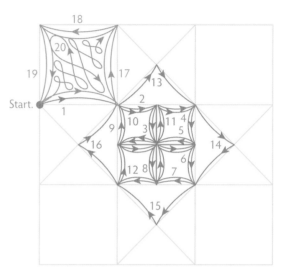

Eight-Pointed Star BLOCKS

The long star points in the Eight-Pointed Star block are perfect for lots of quilting from loops to feathers to continuous curves. This block offers plenty of variety for exploring quilting ideas.

OPTION 1

1. Starting at the lower-left corner of the top-left square, stitch a continuous curved line to the right and into the center square. Stitch curved lines around the inside of the center square. When you reach the top-left corner of the center square, stitch a curved line up the right side of the corner square (purple).

2. Stitch a curved line down to the point of the outer triangle and up to the tip of the next triangle. Working in a clockwise direction, continue stitching curved lines around the star, staying close to the seamlines (green).

3. When you reach the starting point, stitch a curved line along the outer edge of the top-left square. Continue stitching in a clockwise direction around the outer edges of the block (red).

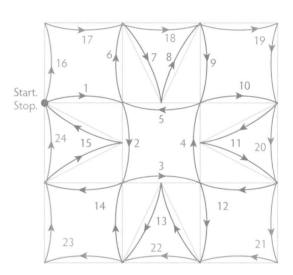

OPTION 2

1. Starting at the tip of the top-left triangle, stitch a continuous curved line down the long side of the triangle. Stitch a curved line up the long side of the next triangle and then down to the corner of the center square. Moving in a clockwise direction, continue stitching the triangles in the same way. Before stitching the long side of the last triangle, stitch curved lines from point to point in the center square (top, red).

2. Stitch curved lines in the last triangle and back to the starting point (bottom, green).

3. Working in a clockwise direction, stitch straight loops across the top triangle, stretching the loops toward the center. Stitch diagonal loops across the corner square. The base of the loops should be along the top and right edges of the square and the loops should stretch toward the center of the block. Continue in the same way until you are back to where you started (bottom, red).

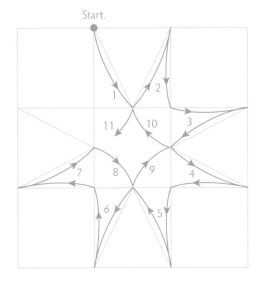

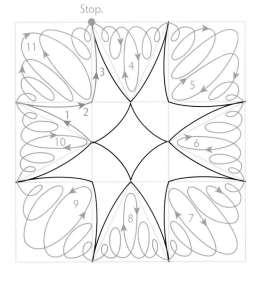

6. Repeat step 4 to stitch two triangles in the lower-left star-point triangle. The triangles don't have to be spaced perfectly; close is good enough. Stitch in the ditch to the top corner of the marked square. Stitch the top-left and top-right triangles in the same way as before. Stitch in the ditch to the next corner of the marked square (bottom, green).

7. Repeat steps 4 and 5 to stitch the star-point triangles and three triangles in the center square (bottom, red).

8. Stitch in the ditch to the last corner of the marked square. Repeat step 4 to stitch the star-point triangles (bottom, red).

OPTION 3

1. Draw an on-point square in the center square. Starting at the lower-left corner of the top-left square, stitch an angled line that reaches toward the outer corner and then goes to the top-right corner of the square. Stitch another angled line that reaches toward the bottom corner and then goes back to the starting point. Stitch a zigzag line inside the diamond shape to travel to the opposite corner (top, purple).

2. Stitch a straight line that echoes the triangle shape to travel to the next corner (top, green).

3. Repeat steps 1 and 2, stitching the squares and triangles in the same way until you reach the starting point (top, red). Tie off.

4. Starting at the left corner of the marked square, stitch along the long side of the top-left triangle. Stitch about two-thirds of the way across the top edge and then back to the starting point. Stitch a smaller triangle in the remaining section of the same triangle (bottom, purple).

5. Using the marked lines as a guide, stitch a triangle in the top-left corner and then the lower-left corner of the center square. Stitch a slightly larger triangle between the corner triangles (bottom, purple).

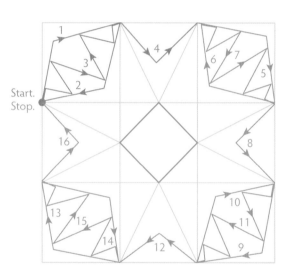

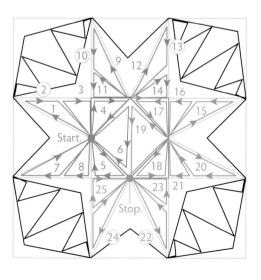

5. Starting at the lower-left corner of the top-left square, stitch a curved line inside the lower triangle. Echo stitch a second curved line to create a double curved line back to the starting point (bottom, green).

6. Stitch feathers that curl toward the outer corner, using the curved line as the spine of the feather. Stitch feathers in the outer triangle, adding a fluffy swirl to reach into the point of the triangle. Continue stitching the corner squares and outer triangles in the same way (bottom, red).

OPTION 4

1. Draw an on-point square in the center square. Then draw two diagonal lines through the on-point square to create four smaller squares. In each corner square, draw a diagonal line from one triangle tip to the opposite tip (blue lines).

2. Starting at the left corner of the marked on-point square and using the marked lines as a guide, stitch double continuous curved lines (page 12) inside each of the smaller squares (top, purple).

3. When you are back to the starting point, stitch swirls that stretch up into the star-point triangle. (I stitched one large swirl with a smaller one on top.) Travel back down the swirl and stitch swirls in the adjacent star-point triangle. Stitch a swirl in the corner of the center square to travel to the top corner of the on-point square (top, green).

4. Repeat step 3, stitching swirls in the same way until you are back to the starting point (top, red). Tie off.

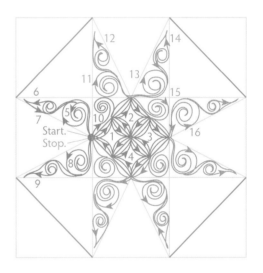

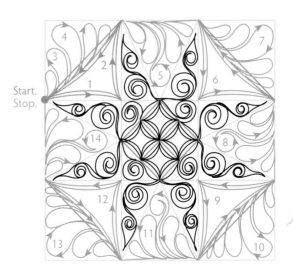

About the Author

Acknowledgments

A huge thank-you to my husband, Rick, and my children, Hannah and Jake. Without your support and encouragement, I never would have written this book.

To my mom, who taught me how to sew and quilt: you're the best.

To my dad, who gifted me my first long-arm machine: your generosity humbles me. You are amazing and I love you.

To Quiltique, the best quilt shop in the universe: I greatly appreciate the fabrics and supplies you donated for my book. You've been very supportive throughout my journey and I love working with you.

Vicki began quilting in 2010 and quickly became addicted. She specializes in custom freehand quilting and computerized edge-to-edge quilting. Her award-winning quilts lean toward a contemporary aesthetic. She has contributed many original designs to *American Patchwork & Quilting, Quilts and More, Make Modern,* and *Modern Quilts Unlimited.* She enjoys teaching and encouraging others to find their quilting voice. Visit Vicki at OrchidOwlQuilts.com.